BIBLE
DOCTRINES

P.C. Nelson

REVISED EDITION

A series of studies based on the
fundamental beliefs of the
Assemblies of God

RadiantBOOKS
Gospel Publishing House/Springfield, Mo 65802

02-0479

DEDICATED

"To the Assembly of God . . .
Sanctified in Christ Jesus,
Called to be saints,
With all who in every place
Call on the name
Of our Lord Jesus Christ,
—Theirs and ours:
Grace unto you and peace
From God our Father
And the Lord Jesus Christ."

First Corinthians 1:2,3
(Translated from the Greek.)

The Assemblies of God doctrinal statements are not reproduced in this revised edition. The *Statement of Fundamental Truths* can be obtained in tract form from Gospel Publishing House.

94   93   92   91   90   89   88   87   8   7   6   5   4

Library of Congress Catalog Card Number 81-82738
International Standard Book Number 0-88243-479-9
Printed in the United States of America

Introduction

This book presents a brief exposition of each of the sixteen sections of the "Statement of Fundamental Truths," the official doctrinal statement of the Assemblies of God.

Adopted originally in 1916—just two years after the formation of the denomination—and remaining unchanged for well over forty years, the Statement was modified slightly by the General Councils of 1961 and 1969. Changes made were in wording and emphasis, not in belief or viewpoint.

The revised section six includes material previously found in sections five and six. Section three, "The Deity of the Lord Jesus Christ," was added in 1961. Sections 10 and 11 were revised and expanded. The changes merely state officially what we have always believed individually.

Because the original author, P. C. Nelson, had passed to his reward by 1961, the exposition on chapter three, "The Deity of the Lord Jesus Christ," was written by J. Roswell Flower, for many years the respected general secretary of this denomination. The new chapters on sections 10 and 11, "The Church and Its Mission" and "The Ministry," were written by Anthony D. Palma, vice-president for academic affairs, Valley Forge Christian College of the Assemblies of God.

3

This book constitutes a convenient guide to the beliefs of the Assemblies of God. It is recommended to all who desire a better acquaintance with "those things most surely believed among us."

November 1981   THOMAS F. ZIMMERMAN
                                 General Superintendent

Contents

1

The Scriptures Inspired

The great Pentecostal movement had its origin in the widespread desire in the hearts of men and women for a closer walk with God, a better understanding of His Word, and for experiences exactly corresponding to the New Testament pattern. It is a reaction against the formalism, coldness, and unbelief prevalent in our times. Pentecostal people, more than others, have experienced the supernatural power of God in their own lives, and with one voice proclaim their faith in the Bible as a supernatural Book, for which, as the infallible, inspired Word of God, they firmly stand.

By the inspiration of the Scriptures we mean that *"special divine influence on the minds of the writers of the Bible, in virtue of which their productions, apart from errors in transcription, and when rightly interpreted, together constitute an infallible rule of faith and practice."*—A. H. Strong.

Paul says to Timothy: "All scripture is *given by inspiration of God,* and is profitable for doctrine, for reproof, for correction, for instruction in righteousness: that the man of God may be perfect, thoroughly furnished unto all good works" (2 Tim. 3:16, 17). In the above text the words, *"given by inspiration of God,"* translate a single word in the Greek—*God-breathed.* The words *"divinely inspired"* (both words coming to us from the Latin) are probably the nearest English equivalent. The German translation says that all Scripture has been *"given in by God,"* and the Swedish says, *"given out by God"*; the Danish says, *"in-blown by God."* God breathed into man what man breathed out.

Peter says that holy men of God spoke "as they were moved [or impelled] by the Holy Ghost." (See Weymouth's rendering of 2 Peter 1:20, 21.*) In Heb. 1:1 we read that God *"spake"* by the prophets and later by His Son. No one can read the Bible attentively without feeling the conviction that all the writers claimed to speak and write by divine authority, as they were directed by the Spirit of God. This makes the Bible God's Book, and different from all other writings in the world.

Let us consider in the briefest way the reasons why we stand for the full inspiration of the Bible:

1. JESUS GAVE THE OLD TESTAMENT HIS FULL SANCTION. He accepted it as the infallible Word of God. "Verily, I say unto you, *Till heaven and earth pass, one jot or one tittle shall in no wise pass from the law, till all be fulfilled"* (Matt. 5:18).

2. THE BOOK IS THE PRODUCT OF ONE MASTER MIND. Sixty-six books, by about forty different writers, living at different places and in different environments during a period of sixteen hundred years;

---

*2 Peter 1:20, 21 (*Weymouth*): "But, above all, remember that no prophecy in Scripture [will be found to have come from the prophet's own prompting]; for never did any prophecy come by human will, but men sent by God spoke as they were impelled by the Holy Spirit."

each, without being aware of it, contributing his essential part to make one whole; each adding to and making clear, but never contradicting what the rest wrote! Such a miracle can be explained only by allowing that there was one Master Mind in control of all these human authors.*

*"Among the writers, 'the holy men of God,' who spoke always inspired by the Holy Spirit, we find persons of various classes and education, since some are priests, as Ezra; poets, as Solomon; prophets, as Isaiah; warriors, as David; shepherds, as Amos; statesmen, as Daniel; sages, as Moses and Paul; and fishermen without letters, as Peter and John. Of these, some formulated laws, as Moses; others wrote history, as Joshua; one wrote psalms, as David; another proverbs, as Solomon; some prophecies, as Jeremiah; others biographies, as the evangelists; others letters, as the apostles.

"In respect to place, the writings were at points as distant as are the sands of Arabia, the deserts of Judea, the porticoes of the temple, the schools of the prophets in Bethel and in Jericho, the palaces of Babylon, on the banks of the Chebar, and in the midst of the Western civilization."—From Eric Lund's *Hermeneutics,* translated from the Spanish by P. C. Nelson.

1 Peter 1:10, 11: "Of which salvation the prophets have inquired and searched diligently, who prophesied of the grace that should come unto you: searching what, or what manner of time the Spirit of Christ which was in them did signify, when it testified beforehand the sufferings of Christ, and the glory that should follow."

Rev. 19:10: "And I fell at his feet to worship him. And he said unto me, See thou do it not: I am thy fellowservant, and of thy brethren that have the testimony of Jesus: worship God: for the testimony of Jesus is the spirit of prophecy."

John 5:39, 46: "Search the scriptures; for in them ye think ye have eternal life: and they are they which testify of me. . . . For had ye believed Moses, ye would have believed me: for he wrote of me."

Luke 24:27: "And beginning at Moses and all the prophets, he expounded unto them in all the scriptures the things concerning himself."

3. THE TYPES, SYMBOLS, AND CEREMONIES ARE EVIDENCES. The verbal predictions concerning Christ are wonderful, but how much more marvelous, the story of Jesus written in the biography of the patriarchs, in the construction of the tabernacle and the temple, and in the services, the sacrifices, and the ceremonies, and in other types and shadows.

4. THE BIBLE PROPHECIES STAMP THE BOOK AS DIVINE. No one but Almighty God, who knows the end from the beginning, could reveal what is so minutely foretold by the prophets concerning individuals, cities, nations, and the world, but most minutely of all concerning the birth, ministry, message, death, and resurrection of Christ and His coming glory (1 Peter 1:10, 11).

5. THE MORAL STANDARDS OF THE BIBLE PROVE IT TO BE DIVINE. The teachings of the Bible constitute the highest moral standard known to man—a standard so high and holy that man without divine aid can never reach it. Some heathen religions have immoral gods, but the God of the Bible dwells in "light which no man can approach unto" (1 Tim. 6:16). Our God can say, "Be ye holy; for I am holy" (1 Peter 1:16). Our Lord will never be satisfied with us till He has wrought out His holiness in us, and we stand approved before Him, without spot or wrinkle or any other blemish (Eph. 5:27). Such a standard is utterly beyond the comprehension of carnal man.

6. THE CREATOR OF MAN IS THE AUTHOR OF THE BOOK. The Bible reveals man to himself and

penetrates to the very center of his being, as no other writing can do. As Weymouth renders Hebrews 4:12: "For the Word of God is full of life and power, and is keener than the sharpest two-edged sword. It pierces even to the severance of soul from spirit, and penetrates between the joints and the marrow, and it can discern the secret thoughts and purposes of the heart."

7. THE BIBLE REVEALS THE ONLY WAY OF SALVATION. God alone can show man the way to forgiveness and cleansing from sin, and deliverance from evil habits and the powers of darkness. In the gospel the way of life is made so plain that the feeblest intellect can understand how to approach God, and the wisest of earth cannot fathom the depth of God's wisdom as seen in the divine plan of salvation. (See Romans 11:33-36.*)

8. THE WORLD RECOGNIZES THE BOOK AS DIVINE. All thinking men put the Bible in a class by itself, and recognize its supernatural character. It is *the Book,* as its very name from the Greek signifies. It has been translated into more languages than any other writing, and is by far the most widely circulated book in the world, and the best-seller. Whole libraries

---

*Rom. 11:33-36: "O the depth of the riches both of the wisdom and knowledge of God! how unsearchable are his judgments, and his ways past finding out! For who hath known the mind of the Lord? or who hath been his counselor? Or who hath first given to him, and it shall be recompensed unto him again? For of him, and through him, and to him are all things: to whom be glory for ever. Amen."

have been written to interpret its sacred pages, and the earth's greatest sages bow in reverence before it.

9. BY ITS FRUITS WE KNOW THE BOOK IS DIVINE. Wherever the Bible has been read, preached, and obeyed, it has transformed individuals and whole nations. Its fruits are always good and wholesome. The neglect of the Word of God means sin, suffering, and sorrow.

10. THE BIBLE WILL OUTLAST THE UNIVERSE. It has withstood all the onslaughts of its enemies, and what is worse, the misinterpretations of its friends. The guns of infidelity have been trained upon it, but not a turret of this mighty castle of truth has fallen.*

---

*Psalm 119:89: "For ever, O Lord, thy word is settled in heaven."

Matt. 5:18: "For verily I say unto you, Till heaven and earth pass, one jot or one tittle shall in no wise pass from the law, till all be fulfilled."

"There is no book that is more persecuted by its enemies, and none more tortured by its friends, than the Bible, due in the final analysis to ignorance of every sound rule of interpretation."—Lund in *Hermeneutics,* page 10.

Keep in mind the fact that it was the Scriptures as they came from the hands of the writers in their original languages that were inspired, and not translations of these Scriptures, however good these translations may be. Contrary to the common view, the oldest translations are not the best. Some of them are translations of translations, as that of John Wycliffe in 1380, which was made from the Latin Vulgate, and not from the original languages. Nevertheless, it was a wonderful help to the cause of Christ, as it was the first English Bible to be put into the hands of the English-speaking people. Other translations appeared which marked distinct advances; and then was brought forth, in 1611, that monumental translation called the King James Version.

11

2

The One True God

The Bible wastes no time in proving the existence of God, and calls the atheist *"the fool."* "The fool hath said in his heart, there is no God" (Psalm 14:1). All races of men have some conception of a god or of gods to whom the human family is accountable. The Bible acquaints us with the true nature and character of the one true and living God. The scriptural delineation of the Supreme Being is the noblest and grandest thought ever conceived by man. Before setting forth the Bible teaching let us clear away some false doctrines concerning God.

1. THE BIBLE IS AGAINST MATERIALISM, that is, the belief that the universe constitutes all the god there is. Many scientists and philosophers have deified matter and laws of nature and have ruled out the eternal God, who is "above all, and through all, and in you all" (Eph. 4:6). Read Isaiah's sublime description of God (chapter 40). The whole material universe is no more to God than the breath you exhale is to you. Jesus said, *"God is a Spirit"* (John 4:24).

2. THE BIBLE IS AGAINST POLYTHEISM, that is the belief in many gods. This is the belief of many millions of people in the world today. It is said that there are over five hundred million people in India, and that there are still more gods in the country

than the whole of the population. "Hear, O Israel: the Lord our God is *one* Lord" (Deuteronomy 6:4).

3. THE BIBLE IS AGAINST PANTHEISM, the belief that "God is all, and all is God." God is not the sum and the spiritual substance of all—an impersonal something, or "the universal mind." God is in all, but also above all, and independent of all, and Jesus is "the express image of his person" (Heb. 1:3), "the image of the invisible God" (Col. 1:15).

4. THE BIBLE IS AGAINST DEISM, the belief that there is a supreme being above us, the source and creator of all things, but so far removed from us that we cannot communicate with Him, and utterly indifferent to our need of Him, and deaf to our cry for mercy and help. "The eyes of the Lord are upon the righteous, and his ears are open unto their cry" (Psalm 34:15). "God is our refuge and strength, a *very present help in trouble*" (Psalm 46:1). Jesus says that not a sparrow could fall to the ground without His Father's notice (Matt. 10:29).

5. "CHRISTIAN THEISM" is the proper name for the Bible doctrine about the Deity. Theism (from the Greek word *Theos,* God) holds that the one true God is present in His universe and that His ear is open to the cry of His children. Christian theism is the sum and substance of the teachings of our Lord Jesus Christ and of His apostles concerning the eternal Godhead.

6. THE GOD OF THE BIBLE IS INFINITE IN HIS PERFECTIONS. He is the uncreated, self-existent,

13

eternal God, the source of all created things. He is omnipotent. By this we mean that there is no limit to His power. He is all-wise and all-knowing—omniscient, as the theologians say. "Thou God, seest me." "He can hear the faintest cry." He is infinite in holiness and love, and dwells in light unapproachable.*

7. JESUS CHRIST IS THE FULL AND FINAL REVELATION OF GOD. He is the radiance of His Father's glory, "the express image of his person" (Heb. 1:3). "No man hath seen God at any time; the only begotten Son, which is in the bosom of the Father, *he hath declared him*" (John 1:18). The Greek word translated "declared" means more than our word to declare or announce. It means to bring what is hidden, mysterious, and obscure into clear light. That is exactly what the Lord Jesus does for this poor, sin-blinded, benighted world. He lived the character of God before our eyes, so that He could say, "He that hath seen me hath seen the Father" (John 14:9).

8. THE GOD OF THE BIBLE IS REVEALED AS A HOLY TRINITY. By this we mean that the Bible sets before us three Divine Persons, named in Scripture, Father, Son, and Holy Spirit; each distinct in office from the others, and yet so perfectly one in character and harmony that they constitute *one God-*

---

*1 Tim. 6:15, 16: "Which in his times he shall show, who is the blessed and only Potentate, the King of kings, and Lord of lords; who only hath immortality, dwelling in the light which no man can approach unto; whom no man hath seen, nor can see: to whom be honor and power everlasting."

head, not three Gods. The doctrine of the Trinity is woven into the Sacred Record and cannot be eliminated without doing violence to the precious Word of God. It is a mystery so profound that the wisest of earth have had to confess their inability to understand it. But praise the Lord, we may know the Father as our Father, the Son as our Brother, and the Holy Spirit as our Advocate. "If a man love me, he will keep my words: and my Father will love him, and *we will come unto him, and make our abode with him*" (John 14:23). In John 14:16, Jesus says, "I will pray the Father, and he shall give you another Comforter [Advocate], that he may abide with you for ever."*

It is well to have a good, scriptural conception of God, but it is not enough to know much *about* Him. The glorious truth revealed to us in Scripture and proved in actual, present-day experience, is that *we may know Him*—have a personal acquaintance with the Mighty God of the universe: "For thus saith the

*The doctrine of the Holy Trinity comes out clearly in nearly all the Books of the New Testament. See how distinctly the three Persons in the Godhead are mentioned in John 14:16: "I will pray THE FATHER, and HE shall give you ANOTHER COMFORTER." The word Advocate is a better translation, and puts us on the track of the right interpretation. Jesus Christ is an Advocate. He is going TO the Father (1 John 2:1), and the Holy Spirit, ANOTHER ADVOCATE, will come FROM the Father. In the Greek the word translated "Advocate" in 1 John 2:1, and "Comforter" in John 14:16, 26; 15:26; and 16:7; is *paraclete*, someone called to the side of one in need of help to aid him as an advocate; one who knows the law and takes the part of the client. Christ is at the Supreme Court of the universe looking after our case there, and the Holy Spirit, as our Advocate, takes charge of us, to instruct, direct, enlighten, and strengthen us.

15

high and lofty One that inhabiteth eternity, whose name is Holy; I dwell in the high and holy place, *with him also that is of a contrite and humble spirit,* to revive the spirit of the humble, and to revive the heart of the contrite ones" (Isa. 57:15). *"Acquaint now thyself with him,* and be at peace: thereby good shall come unto thee" (Job 22:21).

"This is life eternal, that they might know thee the only true God, and Jesus Christ, whom thou hast sent" (John 17:3).

3

The Deity of the Lord Jesus Christ

The Scriptures plainly declare that Jesus Christ was and is the Son of God, as well as the Son of Man. The title "Son of God" is used concerning Him in the New Testament in forty-two or more places. The title "Son of God" belongs to eternity, while the title "Son of Man" belongs specifically to the dimension of time.

It is well to note that God the Father referred to Jesus as His Son (Matt. 3:17; 17:5; Luke 3:22) and that Jesus repeatedly referred to God as His Father (John 5:17). God was and is the Father of Jesus in a peculiar sense, different from the relationship of God to His created offspring (Acts 17:28), for Jesus was declared to be the FIRST begotten (Heb. 1:6) and the ONLY begotten of the Father (John 1:14, 18; 3:16, 18; 1 John 4:9); the term *begotten* having no reference to His birth in Bethlehem, for He was declared to be the FIRST begotten before He was brought into the world (Heb. 1:6).

It is stated in the Scriptures that "in the mouth of two or three witnesses every word may be established" (Matt. 18:16). Witnesses to the sonship of Jesus may be assembled for testimony that is irrefutable.

The prophet Isaiah declared "a child is born" but "a son is given," and his name shall be called, "The mighty God, The everlasting Father, The Prince of Peace" (Isaiah 9:6).

John the Baptist testified that "he that sent me to baptize with water, the same said unto me, Upon whom thou shalt see the Spirit descending, and remaining on him, the same is he which baptizeth with the Holy Ghost. And I saw, and bear record that this is the Son of God" (John 1:33,34).

The disciples bore witness, for as the Lord Jesus began the final stage of His ministry on earth, He asked of His disciples two questions. First, "Whom do men say that I, the Son of man, am?" and, "Whom say ye that I am?" Simon Peter answered the second question without hesitation: "Thou art the Christ, the Son of the living God" (Matt. 16:13-16); and Jesus responded immediately with the assurance that Peter's deduction was correct, that it had been reached, not by his own reasoning, but by the revelation from the Heavenly Father (Matt. 16:17; see John 6:69).

The apostle John referred to Jesus Christ as "the Word" that was "with God" and "was God," and "was made flesh and dwelt among us" (John 1:1,14), and repeatedly thereafter declared Him to be the Son of God (John 1:34).

Jesus was recognized to be the Son of God by evil spirits, but Christ refused to accept their testimony and commanded them to be silent (Mark 3:11,12; Luke 4:41). There was also angelic testimony, for when the angel Gabriel appeared to Mary and informed her she would bear a son, although unmarried, he assured her by declaring: "He shall be great, and shall be called the Son of the Highest," and "that holy thing which shall be born of thee shall be called the Son of God" (Luke 1:32, 35).

Jesus not only received witness from His contemporaries that He was the Son of God, and consented to this witness; He also himself bore witness to His relationship to His Heavenly Father (John 10:36); that He came forth from God and went to God (John 13:3), that He was equal with His Father (John 5:18), and that He and His Father were one (John 10:30, 33).

There is no truth which has been attacked more viciously and with greater persistence than that of the eternal sonship of Jesus. The forty days of temptation in the wilderness were climaxed by the insinuation, twice made by the devil, "If thou be the Son of God." Christ met the temptation and triumphed over it by reference to God's Word.

The temptation was to be repeated in other forms many times thereafter. The claim of the eternal sonship of Jesus was challenged again and again by the scribes and rulers of Judah, and was the basis for the charge of blasphemy which resulted in His condemnation to death.

In the flush of the apostolic ministry and the growth of the Church during the first century, the deity of the Lord Jesus and His eternal sonship, to a great extent, went unchallenged. But the time was to come when the church would be shaken to its foundation by the heresy of one named Arius, a minister of the church in Alexandria.

Arius taught that Christ is a creature halfway between God and man. He was more than human, but less than God. Once (he taught) God lived alone and had no son. Then He created Christ, who in turn created everything else that is.

The teaching of Arius appealed to many of the former pagans who had become converts, for they found it difficult to grasp the Christian belief that Christ has always existed from all eternity and that He is equal with the Father. It seemed to them more reasonable to think of Christ as a kind of divine hero, greater than an ordinary human being, but of lower rank than the eternal God.

A young man, Athanasius by name, later to become the bishop of Alexandria, took issue with Arius, but the controversy became so great that the emperor, Constantine, felt compelled to call a church council to be convened at Nicea on July 4, in A.D. 325. There were leaders in the church who were ready to compromise the truth for the sake of peace, but Athanasius persisted in his fight for the truth, which resulted in the council's finally drawing up a statement to be known as the Nicene Creed, which contained the following statement:

"We believe in one God, the Almighty Father, the creator of all things visible and invisible; and in one Lord Jesus Christ, the Son of God, who alone was begotten of the Father, that is of the substance of the Father, God of God, Light of Light, very God of very God. . . . And in the Holy Ghost."

The issuance of this pronouncement did not finish the Arian heresy for it raged throughout the church for the following fifty years or more before subsiding, and during that period there was dissension, strife, and even bloodshed, as the advocates of the two views came into conflict.

The deity of the Lord Jesus Christ can be summed up concisely. The virgin birth of the Lord Jesus is described in the Scriptures. There seems to have been no question concerning this truth, for nowhere in the Epistles do we find a defense of the virgin birth of Christ. There was need, however, for a defense of the truth of the bodily resurrection of Christ.

The sinless life of Christ is a fact. His temptations were real, but He overcame them all and thus became qualified to serve as a merciful and faithful high priest in things pertaining to God (Heb. 2:17, 18).

His miracles were not questioned, even by His enemies (John 11:47; 12:37). His substitutionary work on the cross is the heart of the gospel, for if Christ had not died for the sins of the people, there would be no hope whatever of salvation. If He had not risen from the dead, then His death on the cross would have been in vain (1 Cor. 15:14). That Christ has been exalted to the right hand of God in heaven, and liveth ever to make intercession for all men, is the hope of all believers and is confirmed by many infallible proofs.

4

The Fall of Man

This twofold subject is too large for adequate treatment here. The most we can do is to build a foundation and indicate profitable lines of study.

1. MAN WAS CREATED IN THE IMAGE AND LIKENESS OF GOD, good and upright, and endowed with intelligence, conscience, and will, so that he could hold dominion over all living things on earth and exercise free choice.*

2. THIS RICH ENDOWMENT OF INTELLIGENCE, CONSCIENCE, AND WILL LIFTED MAN FAR ABOVE THE ANIMAL CREATION, and into fellowship with God. Man's power to choose between good and evil involved the possibility of choosing disobedience and evil instead of obedience and good. Thus his intel-

---

*Gen. 1:26: "And God said, Let us make man in our image, after our likeness: and let them have dominion over the fish of the sea, and over the fowl of the air, and over the cattle, and over all the earth, and over every creeping thing that creepeth upon the earth."

Psalm 8:4-8: "What is man, that thou art mindful of him? and the son of man, that thou visitest him? For thou hast made him a little lower than the angels, and hast crowned him with glory and honor. Thou madest him to have dominion over the works of thy hands; thou hast put all things under his feet: all sheep and oxen, yea, and the beasts of the field; the fowls of the air, and the fish of the sea, and whatsoever passeth through the paths of the seas."

ligence made him fully responsible for all his acts.[1]

3. THE DEVIL, IN THE FORM OF THE SERPENT, RAISED A DOUBT IN THE MIND OF EVE AS TO THE VERACITY OF GOD.

"Yea, hath God said . . . ?" (Genesis 3:1) was the first question ever asked; and our question mark resembles the serpentine coil. "Ye shall not surely die" (v. 4)—a flat contradiction of God's decree—"for God doth know that in the day ye eat thereof, then your eyes shall be opened, and ye shall be as gods, knowing good and evil" (v. 5)—a reflection on the goodness of God.

Eve was enticed by these smooth words and by the inviting appearance of the fruit; she ate and gave to her husband and he ate (v. 6).[2] Thus runs the brief historical statement of the fall of man.

---

[1]Luke 12:47, 48: "And that servant, which knew his lord's will, and prepared not himself, neither did according to his will, shall be beaten with many stripes. But he that knew not, and did commit things worthy of stripes, shall be beaten with few stripes. For unto whomsoever much is given, of him shall be much required; and to whom men have committed much, of him they will ask the more."

Joshua 24:15: "And if it seem evil unto you to serve the Lord, choose you this day whom ye will serve; whether the gods which your fathers served that were on the other side of the flood, or the gods of the Amorites, in whose land ye dwell: but as for me and my house, we will serve the Lord."

[2]Gen. 3:5, 6: "For God doth know that in the day ye eat thereof, then your eyes shall be opened, and ye shall be as gods, knowing good and evil. And when the woman saw that the tree was good for food, and that it was pleasant to the eyes, and a tree to be desired to make one wise, she took of the fruit thereof, and did eat, and gave also unto her husband with her; and he did eat."

4. THE FALL OPENED THE FLOODGATES OF SIN AND SORROW AND SICKNESS AND DEATH UPON THE HUMAN FAMILY.*

---

*Gen. 3:7-24: "And the eyes of them both were opened, and they knew that they were naked; and they sewed fig leaves together, and made themselves aprons.

"And they heard the voice of the Lord God walking in the garden in the cool of the day: and Adam and his wife hid themselves from the presence of the Lord God amongst the trees of the garden. And the Lord God called unto Adam, and said unto him, Where art thou? And he said, I heard thy voice in the garden, and I was afraid, because I was naked; and I hid myself. And he said, Who told thee that thou wast naked? Hast thou eaten of the tree, whereof I commanded thee that thou shouldest not eat? And the man said, The woman whom thou gavest to be with me, she gave me of the tree, and I did eat. And the Lord God said unto the woman, What is this that thou hast done? And the woman said, The serpent beguiled me, and I did eat.

"And the Lord God said unto the serpent, Because thou hast done this, thou art cursed above all cattle, and above every beast of the field; upon thy belly shalt thou go, and dust shalt thou eat all the days of thy life: and I will put enmity between thee and the woman, and between thy seed and her seed; it shall bruise thy head, and thou shalt bruise his heel. Unto the woman he said, I will greatly multiply thy sorrow and thy conception; in sorrow thou shalt bring forth children; and thy desire shall be to thy husband, and he shall rule over thee. And unto Adam he said, Because thou hast hearkened unto the voice of thy wife, and hast eaten of the tree, of which I commanded thee, saying, Thou shalt not eat of it: cursed is the ground for thy sake; in sorrow shalt thou eat of it all the days of thy life; thorns also and thistles shall it bring forth to thee; and thou shalt eat the herb of the field; in the sweat of thy face shalt thou eat bread, till thou return unto the ground; for out of it wast thou taken: for dust thou art, and unto dust shalt thou return.

"And Adam called his wife's name Eve; because she was the mother of all living. Unto Adam also and to his wife did the Lord God make coats of skins, and clothed them.

"And the Lord God said, Behold, the man is become as one of us, to know good and evil; and now, lest he put forth his hand, and take also of the tree of life, and eat, and live for ever:

5. ALL HISTORY AND THE HUMAN CONSCIENCE AND INTELLIGENCE BEAR WITNESS TO THE UNIVERSAL DEPRAVITY OF MAN.

By depravity we mean that man's moral, mental, and spiritual natures have been perverted and distorted by the Fall. Instead of loving holiness, unregenerate man has a vicious bent toward sin and evil, and only the grace of God can overcome this evil nature, by making him a "new creature" in Christ (2 Cor. 5:17).*

---

therefore the Lord God sent him forth from the garden of Eden, to till the ground from whence he was taken. So he drove out the man: and he placed at the east of the garden of Eden cherubim, and a flaming sword which turned every way, to keep the way of the tree of life."

Rom. 5:12-19: "Wherefore, as by one man sin entered into the world, and death by sin; and so death passed upon all men, for that all have sinned: (for until the law sin was in the world: but sin is not imputed when there is no law. Nevertheless death reigned from Adam to Moses, even over them that had not sinned after the similitude of Adam's transgression, who is the figure of him that was to come.

"But not as the offense, so also is the free gift: for if through the offense of one many be dead, much more the grace of God, and the gift by grace, which is by one man, Jesus Christ, hath abounded unto many. And not as it was by one that sinned, so is the gift: for the judgment was by one to condemnation, but the free gift is of many offenses unto justification. For if by one man's offense death reigned by one; much more they which receive abundance of grace and of the gift of righteousness shall reign in life by one, Jesus Christ.)

"Therefore, as by the offense of one judgment came upon all men to condemnation; even so by the righteousness of one the free gift came upon all men unto justification of life. For as by one man's disobedience many were made sinners, so by the obedience of one shall many be made righteous."

1 Cor. 15:21: "For since by man came death, by man came also the resurrection of the dead."

*2 Cor. 5:17: "Therefore if any man be in Christ, he is a new creature: old things are passed away; behold, all things are become new."

This depravity affects man's mental or intellectual nature, which has been perverted, so that men became "vain in their imaginations, and their foolish heart [mind] was darkened. Professing themselves to be wise, they became fools" (Rom. 1:21, 22).[1] They became men of a "reprobate mind" and "without understanding" (Rom. 1:28, 31).[2] Men have lost the power of distinguishing good from evil (Isa. 5:20),[3] and some have descended below the level of brutes and "glory in their shame," resembling the waters

---

The Greek word translated "creature" is significant. The literal meaning is "creation." Moffatt, in his free translation, renders it thus: "There is a new creation whenever a man comes to be in Christ: what is old has gone, the new has come."

Paul uses the word "workmanship," His make, His "handiwork, in Ephesians 2:10 (*Weymouth*). The word above translated "new" means something different, unheard of, not experienced before. It appears in the noun form in Rom. 6:4 and 7:6. This conforms to our own experience.

The word "depravity" comes to us from the Latin, and its root meaning is crooked, distorted, twisted out of shape, and from that comes to mean morally bad, wicked. God made man "good and upright." The devil came in and ruined, spoiled, defiled the beautiful work of God, and man became a degenerate, depraved being, unlike man in his original state.

[1]Rom. 1:21, 22: "Because that, when they knew God, they glorified him not as God, neither were thankful; but became vain in their imaginations, and their foolish heart was darkened. Professing themselves to be wise, they became fools."

[2]Rom. 1:28, 31: "And even as they did not like to retain God in their knowledge, God gave them over to a reprobate mind, to do those things which are not convenient [fitting]; ... without understanding, covenant-breakers, without natural affection, implacable, unmerciful."

[3]Isa. 5:20: "Woe unto them that call evil good, and good evil; that put darkness for light and light for darkness; that put bitter for sweet, and sweet for bitter!"

of the restless sea, "[casting] up mire and dirt" (Isa. 57:20).

The unregenerate state of man is portrayed with photographic precision in Romans 3:9-18.[1] (Compare this with Rom. 1:18-32.) Phil. 3:19 (Moffatt) reads: "Destruction is their fate, the belly is their god, they glory in their shame, these men of earthly mind!"

6. THIS DEPRAVITY TOUCHES MAN'S WHOLE BEING —his mental, moral, spiritual and physical natures. It is absolutely universal.[2]

Man as we know him is not evolved from the

---

[1]Rom. 3:9-18: "What then? are we better than they? No, in no wise: for we have before proved both Jews and Gentiles, that they are all under sin; as it is written, There is none righteous, no, not one: there is none that understandeth, there is none that seeketh after God. They are all gone out of the way, they are together become unprofitable; there is none that doeth good, no, not one. Their throat is an open sepulchre; with their tongues they have used deceit; the poison of asps is under their lips: whose mouth is full of cursing and bitterness: their feet are swift to shed blood: destruction and misery are in their ways: and the way of peace have they not known: there is no fear of God before their eyes." (Compare with Romans 1:18-32.)

[2]Rom. 3:19: "Now we know that what things soever the law saith, it saith to them who are under the law: that every mouth may be stopped, and all the world may become guilty before God."

Everyone knows that he is not what he ought to be and cannot be what he wants to be, except by the grace of God. All know that there is something wrong with the human family, and that man's whole bent or tendency is in the direction of evil, and that it takes a brave fight to develop a highly moral character, such as all admire. The newspapers are full of evidence of man's depravity. We do not need to be taught to sin, for we are "by nature" (birth) "the children of wrath"—children exposed to the wrath of God on account of our sinful nature—"And you did he animals but he came perfect from the hands of God, and is a depraved, degenerate creature, estranged from God, and in sin and rebellion, under the just condemnation of a holy God.

7. CHRIST, OUR REDEEMER, WAS TEMPTED IN ALL POINTS AS WE ARE.*

---

make alive, when ye were dead through your trespasses and sins, wherein ye once walked . . . according to the prince of the powers of the air, of the spirit that now worketh in the sons of disobedience"—this describes the Gentiles—"among whom we [Jews] also all once lived in the lusts of our flesh, doing the desires of the flesh and of the mind, and were by nature children of wrath, even as the rest" (Eph. 2:1-3, *ASV*).

*Matt. 4:1-11: "Then was Jesus led up of the Spirit into the wilderness to be tempted of the devil. And when he had fasted forty days and forty nights, he was afterward ahungered. And when the tempter came to him, he said, If thou be the Son of God, command that these stones be made bread. But he answered and said, It is written, Man shall not live by bread alone, but by every word that proceedeth out of the mouth of God.

"Then the devil taketh him up into the holy city, and setteth him on a pinnacle of the temple, and saith unto him, If thou be the Son of God, cast thyself down: for it is written, He shall give his angels charge concerning thee: and in their hands they shall bear thee up, lest at any time thou dash thy foot against a stone. Jesus said unto him, It is written again, Thou shalt not tempt the Lord thy God.

"Again, the devil taketh him up into an exceeding high mountain, and showeth him all the kingdoms of the world, and the glory of them; and saith unto him, All these things will I give thee, if thou wilt fall down and worship me. Then saith Jesus unto him, Get thee hence, Satan: for it is written, Thou shalt worship the Lord thy God, and him only shalt thou serve. Then the devil leaveth him, and behold, angels came and ministered unto him."

Heb. 4:15: "For we have not a high priest which cannot be touched with the feeling of our infirmities; but was in all points tempted like as we are, yet without sin."

He paid the full price of our ransom,[1] became the propitiation for the sins of the whole world,[2] was made sin for us, though He was sinless,[3] and by His sacrificial death made a full atonement for all our sins.[4]

8. MAN'S SIN AND SHAME AND GOD'S REDEEMING GRACE ARE THE SUM AND SUBSTANCE OF THE BIBLE.

As man's iniquity is unfathomable, so is God's grace: "Where sin abounded, grace did much more abound" (Rom. 5:20).

We praise God that the divine plan of redemption reaches the lowest sinner, and lifts the believer into

---

[1]Matt. 20:28: "Even as the Son of man came not to be ministered unto, but to minister, and to give his life a ransom for many."

[2]1 John 2:2: "And he is the propitiation for our sins: and not for ours only, but also for the sins of the whole world."

[3]2 Cor. 5:21: "For he hath made him to be sin for us, who knew no sin; that we might be made the righteousness of God in him."

[4]Rom. 5:6-11,20,21: "For when we were yet without strength, in due time Christ died for the ungodly. For scarcely for a righteous man will one die: yet peradventure for a good man some would even dare to die. But God commendeth his love toward us, in that, while we were yet sinners, Christ died for us. Much more then, being now justified by his blood, . . . we shall be saved by his life. And not only so, but we also joy in God through our Lord Jesus Christ, by whom we have now received the atonement. . . . Moreover the law entered, that the offense might abound. But where sin abounded, grace did much more abound: that as sin hath reigned unto death, even so might grace reign through righteousness unto eternal life by Jesus Christ our Lord."

Eph. 1:7: "In whom we have redemption through his blood, the forgiveness of sins, according to the riches of his grace."

a life of victory, happiness, holiness, and eternal bliss, and that it extends to spirit, soul, and body, and even to nature, which came under the curse of sin (Gen. 3:7-19; Rom. 8:19-23).*

*Rom. 8:19-23: "For the earnest expectation of the creature waiteth for the manifestation of the sons of God. For the creature was made subject to vanity, not willingly, but by reason of him who hath subjected the same in hope; because the creature itself also shall be delivered from the bondage of corruption into the glorious liberty of the children of God. For we know that the whole creation groaneth and travaileth in pain together until now. And not only they, but ourselves also, which have the firstfruits of the Spirit, even we ourselves groan within ourselves, waiting for the adoption, to wit, the redemption of our body."

5

The Salvation of Man

The subject is treated in the large works on doctrine at great length under the heading of "Soteriology." It would be impossible to give here more than a few hints to indicate the lines for a lifetime of careful study.

This great word, *salvation*, is the theme of the whole Bible, and the theme of every gospel sermon. The great hymns of the church almost without exception sing of the great salvation wrought by Jesus Christ. C. I. Scofield's definition is so comprehensive that it is worth committing to memory: "The Hebrew and Greek words for salvation," says this gifted author in his comment on Romans 1:16, "imply the ideas of deliverance, safety, preservation, healing, and soundness. Salvation is the great inclusive word of the gospel, gathering into itself all the redemptive acts and processes: as justification, redemption, grace, propitiation, imputation, forgiveness, sanctification, and glorification."

Conditions to Salvation

Let us see if we can clarify this great theme by giving you a few simple propositions in everyday speech:

1. SALVATION IS FROM GOD AND NOT FROM MAN.*

---

*Luke 3:6: "And all flesh shall see the salvation of God."

It was thought by God the Father, bought by the Son, and wrought by the Spirit, and man had no part in planning it or purchasing it. His part is to accept it as a gift from God.[1] As soon as man sinned, our God announced His great plan of salvation.[2]

2. SALVATION IS THROUGH CHRIST ALONE.[3]

As Peter, under the anointing of the Holy Spirit, told the Jewish senate, it is *salvation through Christ or damnation without Him.* Christ came to seek and to save the lost (Luke 19:10). He came to give His life a *ransom for many* (Matt. 20:28). He is the *propitiation* for our sins, and for the sins of the whole world (1 John 2:2). By Him we have received the *atonement* (Rom. 5:11). "We have *redemption* through his blood, the *forgiveness* of sins, according to the riches of his grace" (Eph. 1:7). "*Without shedding of blood is no remission*" (Heb. 9:22).

3. SALVATION IS OBTAINED BY GRACE AND NOT BY WORKS.[4]

---

[1]Rom. 6:23: "For the wages of sin is death; but the gift of God is eternal life through Jesus Christ our Lord."

Luke 19:10: "For the Son of man is come to seek and to save that which was lost."

[2]Gen. 3:15: "And I will put enmity between thee and the woman, and between thy seed and her seed; it shall bruise thy head, and thou shalt bruise his heel."

[3]Acts 4:12: "Neither is there salvation in any other: for there is none other name under heaven given among men, whereby we must be saved."

[4]Eph. 2:8-10: "For by grace are ye saved through faith; and that not of yourselves: it is the gift of God: not of works, lest any man should boast. For we are his workmanship, created in Christ Jesus unto good works, which God hath before ordained that we should walk in them."

We are not able to save ourselves by our own good works, as is so clearly taught in this and other writings of Paul. It is wholly of *grace*. In Romans, Paul argues that the Gentiles, who have not the direct revelation from God (the Law), are lost because they have failed to follow the light they have (chapter 1), and the Jews, who have the Law, have failed to walk in the light they have (chapter 2). Thus, he concludes all the world is guilty before God, and lost—"that every mouth may be stopped, and *all the world may become guilty before God. Therefore by the deeds of the law there shall no flesh be justified in his sight*" (Rom. 3:19, 20). The clear perception of this truth by Martin Luther started the Reformation in Europe. Alas for Protestantism! Millions of Protestants are now in darkness concerning this truth, and are trying to "be good enough to be saved"—trying to save themselves in whole or in part, instead of flinging themselves in their helplessness on One who alone can save (Rom. 10:2-4).

4. SALVATION IS FOR THE WHOLE MAN (Isaiah 53:1-10; Rom. 8:19-23).*

Salvation is not merely the forgiveness of our sins,

---

*Isa. 53:1-10: "Who hath believed our report? and to whom is the arm of the Lord revealed? For he shall grow up before him as a tender plant, and as a root out of a dry ground: he hath no form or comeliness; and when we shall see him, there is no beauty that we should desire him. He is despised and rejected of men; a man of sorrows, and acquainted with grief: and we hid as it were our faces from him; he was despised, and we esteemed him not. Surely he hath borne our griefs, and carried our sorrows: yet we did esteem him stricken, smitten of God, and afflicted. But he was wounded for our transgressions, he was bruised for

33

and justification before God's court. It includes cleansing and keeping, and, shown in the definition quoted at the beginning of this chapter, it includes healing from bodily infirmities, as plainly taught by Isaiah, in chapters 35 and 53, and in other Scripture passages. In Romans 8 Paul shows that Christ's redemption extends to the removal of the curse that rests like a pall on the whole creation, both animate and inanimate. For man's sake the very ground came under a curse (Gen. 3:17-19). The animal creation as well as man has suffered much on account of man's sin, but Christ was made a curse for us (Gal. 3:13), and He will yet lift the curse from the whole creation.*

---

our iniquities: the chastisement of our peace was upon him; and with his stripes we are healed. All we like sheep have gone astray; we have turned every one to his own way; and the Lord hath laid on him the iniquity of us all. He was oppressed, and he was afflicted, yet he opened not his mouth: he is brought as a lamb to the slaughter, and as a sheep before her shearers is dumb, so he openeth not his mouth. He was taken from prison and from judgment: and who shall declare his generation? for he was cut off out of the land of the living: for the transgression of my people was he stricken. And he made his grave with the wicked, and with the rich in his death; because he had done no violence, neither was any deceit in his mouth. Yet it pleased the Lord to bruise him; he hath put him to grief: when thou shalt make his soul an offering for sin, he shall see his seed, he shall prolong his days, and the pleasure of the Lord shall prosper in his hand.''

Rom. 8:19-23 is quoted on page 30.

*Isa. 11:6-9: ''The wolf also shall dwell with the lamb, and the leopard shall lie down with the kid; and the calf and the young lion and the fatling together; and a little child shall lead them. And the cow and the bear shall feed; their young ones shall lie down together: and the lion shall eat straw like the ox. And the sucking child shall play on the hole of the asp, and the

Matthew 8:17[1] correctly translates Isaiah 53:4, showing that Christ is a Saviour from sickness as well as a Saviour from sin. To this great truth earth is gradually awakening now again, as multitudes did when Christ walked the shores of Galilee.

5. SALVATION IS FOR TIME AND ETERNITY.[2]

As the author of the Paragraph Bible says, salvation is in three tenses—past, present, and future. We have been saved from the guilt and penalty of sin.[3] We are being saved from the habit, power, and dominion of sin.[4] We are to be saved not

---

weaned child shall put his hand on the cockatrice' den. They shall not hurt nor destroy in all my holy mountain: for the earth shall be full of the knowledge of the Lord, as the waters cover the sea."

[1]Matt. 8:17: "That it might be fulfilled which was spoken by Isaiah the prophet, saying, Himself took our infirmities, and bare our sicknesses."

[2]Heb. 5:9: "And being made perfect, he became the author of eternal salvation unto all them that obey him."

[3]2 Cor. 2:15: "For we are unto God a sweet savor of Christ, in them that are saved, and in them that perish."

Eph. 2:5, 8: "Even when we were dead in sins, hath quickened us together with Christ (by grace ye are saved;). . . . For by grace are ye saved through faith; and that not of yourselves: it is the gift of God."

2 Tim. 1:9: "Who hath saved us, and called us with a holy calling, not according to our works, but according to his own purpose and grace, which was given us in Christ Jesus before the world began."

Eph. 1:7: "In whom we have redemption through his blood, the forgiveness of sins, according to the riches of his grace."

[4]Rom. 6:14: "For sin shall not have dominion over you: for ye are not under the law, but under grace."

Phil. 2:12,13: "Wherefore, my beloved, as ye have always obeyed, not as in my presence only, but now much more in my

35

only from the penalty, pollution, and power of sin, but also from the presence and consequences of sin. "Now is our salvation nearer than when we believed" (Rom. 13:11). "Who are kept by the power of God through faith unto salvation ready to be revealed in the last time" (1 Peter 1:5).

At His coming, Christ will change our corruptible bodies to be like His glorious body.[1] Not a trace of the effects of sin will remain in us, and the whole "earth shall be full of the knowledge of the Lord, as the waters cover the sea" (Isaiah 11:9). That will be *full salvation.*

6. SALVATION IS NEGLECTED AT FEARFUL COST.[2]

The sin of sins is unbelief and rejection of Christ.

---

absence, work out your own salvation with fear and trembling: For it is God which worketh in you both to will and to do of his good pleasure."

2 Cor. 3:18: "But we all, with open face beholding as in a glass the glory of the Lord, are changed into the same image from glory to glory, even as by the Spirit of the Lord."

[1]Phil. 3:20, 21: "For our conversation is in heaven; from whence also we look for the Saviour, the Lord Jesus Christ: who shall change our vile body, that it may be fashioned like unto his glorious body, according to the working whereby he is able even to subdue all things unto himself."

[2]Heb. 2:1-4: "Therefore we ought to give the more earnest heed to the things which we have heard, lest at any time we should let them slip. For if the word spoken by angels was steadfast, and every transgression and disobedience received a just recompense of reward; how shall we escape, if we neglect so great salvation; which at the first began to be spoken by the Lord, and was confirmed unto us by them that heard him; God also bearing them witness, both with signs and wonders, and with divers miracles, and gifts of the Holy Ghost, according to his own will?"

This is the sin which causes the wrath of God to abide upon a lost soul.[1] Unbelief makes God a liar.[2] It is a gross sin even to *neglect so great a salvation,* and this neglect pulls down on the head of the impenitent a punishment more terrible than death (Heb. 2:2, 3; 10:28, 29).[3]

7. FAITH IN CHRIST AS OUR CRUCIFIED AND RISEN SAVIOUR AND LORD IS THE PROCURING CAUSE OF SALVATION, AS UNBELIEF IS OF DAMNATION.

This is most clearly brought out in John 3:14-36. "Whosoever believeth in him should not perish, but have eternal life" (verse 15); repeated in verse 16, ". . . but have everlasting life"; and in verse 36, "He

---

[1]John 3:18-21, 36: "He that believeth on him is not condemned: but he that believeth not is condemned already, because he hath not believed in the name of the only begotten Son of God. And this is the condemnation, that light is come into the world, and men loved darkness rather than light, because their deeds were evil. For every one that doeth evil hateth the light, neither cometh to the light, lest his deeds should be reproved. But he that doeth truth cometh to the light, that his deeds may be made manifest, that they are wrought in God."

"He that believeth on the Son hath everlasting life: and he that believeth not the Son shall not see life; but the wrath of God abideth on him."

[2]1 John 5:10: "He that believeth on the Son of God hath the witness in himself: he that believeth not God hath made him a liar; because he believeth not the record that God gave of his Son."

[3]Heb. 10:28, 29: "He that despised Moses' law died without mercy under two or three witnesses: of how much sorer punishment, suppose ye, shall he be thought worthy, who hath trodden under foot the Son of God, and hath counted the blood of the covenant, wherewith he was sanctified, an unholy thing, and hath done despite unto the Spirit of grace?"

that believeth on the Son hath everlasting life."
(Compare this with John 5:24.) The same Greek
word is used in the four verses and is translated
"eternal" once and "everlasting" three times.
"Being justified by faith" (Rom. 5:1). "For by grace
are ye saved *through faith*" (Eph. 2:8).

But the faith that saves presupposes genuine
repentance, and is followed by obedience: *"Repent
ye,* and *believe* the gospel" (Mark 1:15). "Obedience
to the faith" (Rom. 1:5). "Obedience of faith" (Rom.
16:26). "Repent, and be baptized every one of you"
(Acts 2:38). Repentance is evidenced by confession
(followed by reformation) and procures forgiveness
and cleansing.[1]

8. The Father, the Son, and the Holy Spirit
Cooperate With the Sinner in His
Salvation.

In the above statements we have been looking at
salvation from the human side—manward. We must
confess and forsake sin;[2] we must seek the Lord and
turn to the Lord, and He will have mercy on us, and
will abundantly pardon.[3] But there is also a
Godward side to salvation. The Father draws the

---

[1] 1 John 1:7: "But if we walk in the light, as he is in the light, we
have fellowship one with another, and the blood of Jesus Christ
his Son cleanseth us from all sin."

[2] Prov. 28:13: "He that covereth his sins shall not prosper, but
whoso confesseth and forsaketh them shall have mercy."

[3] Isa. 55:6, 7: "Seek ye the Lord while he may be found, call ye
upon him while he is near: Let the wicked forsake his way, and
the unrighteous man his thoughts: and let him return unto the
Lord, and he will have mercy upon him; and to our God, for he
will abundantly pardon."

sinner.[1] The Holy Spirit convicts the sinner,[2] and the sinner is regenerated by the power of the Spirit—is "born of the Spirit," "born again."[3] In regeneration we become partakers of the divine nature, enabling us to escape "the corruption that is in the world through lust" (2 Peter 1:4). This divine nature in us will expel all desire for sin, and cause us to love holiness and to seek after it: "Whosoever is born of God doth not commit sin [does not make a practice of sinning]; for his seed [the divine life implanted in him] remaineth in him: and he cannot sin [live in sin], because he is born of God" (1 John 3:9, interpreted in the light of other parts of the same Epistle).

The Evidences of Salvation

The evidences are both inward (subjective) and outward (objective). The newborn babe in Christ is

---

[1]John 6:44: "No man can come to me, except the Father which hath sent me draw him: and I will raise him up at the last day."

[2]John 16:8: "And when he is come, he will reprove the world of sin, and of righteousness, and of judgment."

[3]John 1:11,12: "He came unto his own, and his own received him not. But as many as received him, to them gave he power to become the sons of God, even to them that believe on his name."

John 3:3-7: "Jesus answered and said unto him, Verily, verily, I say unto thee, Except a man be born again, he cannot see the kingdom of God. Nicodemus saith unto him, How can a man be born when he is old? can he enter a second time into his mother's womb, and be born? Jesus answered, Verily, verily, I say unto thee, Except a man be born of water and of the Spirit, he cannot enter into the kingdom of God. That which is born of the flesh is flesh; and that which is born of the Spirit is spirit. Marvel not that I said unto thee, Ye must be born again."

apt to lay emphasis on the lifting of the burden of sin under conviction,* and the new joy which flooded his soul when he became conscious of forgiveness and cleansing, "the joy of salvation": "Make me to hear joy and gladness; that the bones which thou hast broken may rejoice" (Psalm 51:8; see also v. 12). He may tell the story in terms of feeling, but feelings must rest on solid faith in something substantial and unchanging—the promises of God in the Word of God.

When the sinner repents and believes, and accepts Christ by faith as his personal Saviour, his spirit witnesses to his new experience of salvation through Christ, and the Spirit, as a corroborative witness, *bears witness with his spirit* that he is a child of God. As Christians, we begin to call God *"our Father"*; something we could not do before. "We cry, Abba, Father" (Romans 8:15,16). The word *abba* is from the Aramaic (the language spoken by the Jews in Palestine at the time of Jesus) and means *Father*. Paul turns this into Greek and the translators turn it into English.

John, the apostle of love, cites another inward evidence: "Every one that loveth is born of God, and knoweth God" (1 John 4:7). "We know that we

---

*Psalm 32:3-6: "When I kept silence, my bones waxed old through my roaring all day long. For day and night thy hand was heavy upon me: my moisture is turned into the drought of summer. Selah. I acknowledged my sin unto thee, and mine iniquity have I not hid. I said, I will confess my transgressions unto the Lord; and thou forgavest the iniquity of my sin. Selah. For this shall every one that is godly pray unto thee in a time when thou mayest be found: surely in the floods of great waters they shall not come nigh unto him."

have passed from death unto life, *because we love the brethren*" (1 John 3:14).

God gives us still another inward evidence, the impartation of the Holy Spirit—"Hereby know we that we dwell in him, and he in us, *because he hath given us of his Spirit*" (1 John 4:13).

The outward evidence—a life of obedience to the law and will of God, a life of holiness lived by the power of the indwelling Christ, reproducing His own life in us, empowering us for service, and fitting us for heaven—is apparent to the believer himself and to all who know him. The Scripture passages concerning the outward evidence are so numerous that anyone can easily find them in abundance; hence, we will not cite them here.

6

The Ordinances of the Church

Baptism in Water

There are four questions that are frequently asked concerning the ordinance of baptism: (1) What was the *mode* of baptism in Bible times? (2) What is the significance, or *symbolism,* of baptism? (3) What is the right *formula* for administering the ordinance? and, (4) Who is scripturally *qualified* to be baptized? Let us consider these questions in the order given.

The Mode

More properly, the *act* of baptism. There is great confusion on this subject because too many follow tradition instead of the Bible.

The Assemblies of God, as well as most of the other Pentecostal groups, practices immersion in water in the name of the Father, Son, and Holy Spirit.

The experience of being baptized in the Holy Spirit makes us so pliable in the hands of God that we are willing to receive instructions direct from the Word of God on this subject as on all others; we have been loosed from the bonds of tradition.

Suppose a Bible were dropped on an island which had never been touched by a missionary, and that the natives were able to read and understand this

42

Bible, and that some of them were actually converted by reading this Book, and therefore desired to do all the will of God. A diligent reading of the New Testament would show that believers were to be baptized. But they have never seen anyone baptized and must learn from the Bible how it is to be done. They would soon discover:

1. That the ordinance requires *water*: "And as they went on their way, they came unto a certain water: and the eunuch said, See, here is *water*; what doth hinder me to be baptized?" (Acts 8:36).

2. That baptism requires *much* water: "And John also was baptizing in Aenon, near to Salim, *because there was much water there*: and they came, and were baptized" (John 3:23).

3. That baptism requires the administrator and the candidate to go *down into* the water: "And they *went down both into the water, both Philip and the eunuch;* and he baptized him" (Acts 8:38).

4. That baptism requires *a burial in water:* "Therefore we are *buried* with him by baptism into death" (Rom. 6:4). *"Buried* with him in baptism" (Col. 2:12).

5. That baptism requires a *coming up out of* the water: "And Jesus, when he was baptized, went up straightway out of the water" (Matt. 3:16). "And when they were come up out of the water . . . " (Acts 8:39).

The Symbolism

This was beautiful and wonderful. It pictures the death, burial, and resurrection of Christ, and of the believer in fellowship with Him.

"Therefore we are buried with him by baptism into death: that like as Christ was raised up from the dead by the glory of the Father, even so we also should walk in newness of life. For if we have been planted together in the likeness of his *death*, we shall be also in the likeness of his *resurrection*" (Rom. 6:4, 5). "*Buried* with him in baptism, wherein also ye are *risen* with him" (Col. 2:12).

As most great scholars of all branches of Christendom, even those who practice infant baptism and sprinkling and pouring, specifically declare, the original mode was *immersion*, as the Greek words translated "baptism" and "baptize" clearly signify.* Moreover, nearly all the translations into modern languages convey the same meaning. It is no more difficult for a

---

*The literature on the subject of baptism is abundant. The controversy about the mode of baptism has raged in Protestantism from the days of Luther, Zwingli, and Calvin. Many great and learned works have been published. One of the best is by J. Gilchrist Lawson. It is entitled, *Did Jesus Command Immersion?* The whole volume is devoted to proving that the Greek words translated baptize and baptism mean to immerse and immersion. To do this the author quotes from fifteen English dictionaries; six English etymological dictionaries; twenty-five encyclopedias; twenty Bible dictionaries; twenty religious encyclopedias; one hundred Greek lexicons; forty-six classical Greek writers, from Orpheus (1,000 B.C.) to Eustathius (A.D. 1,000); nineteen early Christian writers, from Barnabas in the latter part of the first century to Theophylact, 11th century; twelve versions of the N.T., including Syriac, Arabic, Egyptian, Ethiopic, Latin, Gothic, Armenian, Anglo-Saxon, Persic, Slavic, Welsh, Irish, and Gaelic versions; seventy famous commentaries; thirty-two noted theologians; and fifty-three great historians.

This is followed by testimonies of representatives of Greek, Roman Catholic, Lutheran, Episcopal, Methodist, Presbyterian, Quaker, and other churches. The argument is simply overwhelming. (This book is now out of print.)

Greek scholar to tell you the meaning of the words used in the Greek New Testament for this ordinance than it is for an Englishman to tell the meaning of the word *dip* or *immerse*.

Fidelity to Christ demands that we do exactly what His Word teaches, and that we do not substitute some other "mode." In loyalty to the Lord we must keep the ordinances as they were delivered to us by the apostles.

The Formula

Our Lord himself gave His apostles the formula in Matthew 28:18,19, which Worrell in his excellent original translation of the New Testament correctly renders thus: "All authority was given to Me in heaven and on earth: going, therefore, disciple ye all the nations, immersing them into the name of the Father, and of the Son, and of the Holy Spirit; teaching them to observe all things, whatsoever I commanded you; and, behold, I am with you all the days, even to the end of the age."

We are not left to speculate on the proper formula—"*into* the name of the Father, and of the Son, and of the Holy Spirit."* The American

---

*Great injury to the cause of Christ, and in particular to the cause of the very doctrines for which the Pentecostal people stand, is done by those who hold and declare that we must be baptized in the name of "Jesus only" and that those who have been "baptized into the name of the Father, the Son, and the Holy Ghost," as Jesus himself commanded, have not been scripturally baptized. This is a dangerous error which has been brought forward for the purpose of denying the Biblical doctrine of the Holy Trinity.

Standard Version, as well as Worrell's translation, has *into*, instead of *in*, and this is the correct translation from the Greek. Into fellowship with the name of the Holy Trinity—and we do this in the name of (by the authority and command of) Jesus Christ.

The Candidates

Before leaving this fascinating study, let us consider the proper candidates or subjects for baptism. The divine order is very simple. The sinner must first repent and believe (Mark 1:15; Acts 2:38). Believers, and believers only, are to be baptized (Matt. 28:19; Mark 16:16). This excludes children who are too young to repent and believe, and invalidates the "baptism" of those who were not regenerated when they submitted to the ordinance. Does this explain why the twelve men at Ephesus were rebaptized by Paul?*

Some hold that the baptism in the Holy Spirit precludes the necessity of submitting to this

---

*Acts 19:1-7: "And it came to pass, that, while Apollos was at Corinth, Paul having passed through the upper coasts came to Ephesus; and finding certain disciples, he said unto them, Have ye received the Holy Ghost since ye believed? And they said unto him, We have not so much as heard whether there be any Holy Ghost. And he said unto them, Unto what then were ye baptized? And they said, Unto John's baptism. Then said Paul, John verily baptized with the baptism of repentance, saying unto the people, that they should believe on him which should come after him, that is, on Christ Jesus. When they heard this, they were baptized in the name of the Lord Jesus. And when Paul had laid his hands upon them, the Holy Ghost came on them; and they spake with tongues, and prophesied. And all the men were about twelve."

ordinance. This position is flatly contradicted by Peter.[1]

If you will read through the New Testament to see what stress was laid upon the ordinance, you will be struck with the suddenness with which believers were baptized after conversion, and the great emphasis placed on the ordinance by Christ and the apostles.[2]

Holy Communion

This holy ordinance symbolizes the broken body

---

[1]Acts 10:47, 48: "Can any man forbid water, that these should not be baptized, which have received the Holy Ghost as well as we? And he commanded them to be baptized in the name of the Lord. Then prayed they him to tarry certain days."

[2]Note in particular the following passages:

Acts 2:38,41: "Repent, and be baptized every one of you. . . . Then they that gladly received his word were baptized: and the *same day* there were added unto them about three thousand souls."

Acts 8:12: "When they believed Philip preaching . . . they were baptized." (See also v. 13.)

Acts 8:36,38: "They came unto a certain water: and the eunuch said, See, here is water; what doth hinder me to be baptized? . . . And he commanded the chariot to stand still: and they went down both into the water, both Philip and the eunuch; and he baptized him."

Acts 9:18: "And he [Saul or Paul] received sight forthwith, and arose, and was baptized." Compare this with Acts 22:16: "And now why tarriest thou? arise, and be baptized, and wash away thy sins."

Acts 10:47,48: "Can any man forbid water, that these should not be baptized . . . ? And he commanded them to be baptized." (Note that this was the very first service that Peter held in the home of Cornelius, and that he *commanded* them to be baptized.)

Acts 16:14,15: "Lydia . . . heard us: whose heart the Lord opened, that she attended unto the things which were spoken of Paul. And when she was baptized. . . ."

47

and the shed blood of our Lord, our participation in the benefits of His atoning death, and the covenant which He sealed with His own blood. It represents our union with Him who is the sustenance of our spiritual life. It is a memorial of His death, and looks forward to His coming again.

1. THE ORDINANCE WAS INSTITUTED BY OUR LORD HIMSELF[1] on the very eve of His betrayal.[2] Let us with bowed heads approach the Upper Room where Christ and His apostles, reclining around the table, were observing for the last time together the Paschal Supper, which prefigured His sacrificial death as "the Lamb of God, which taketh away the sin of the world" (John 1:29), and instituted this memorial ordinance, which was ever to point back to the death of our Lord on the cross, and forward to His coming again in the clouds of glory. The words spoken on this occasion seem to have been few, but came from the depth of our Saviour's heart and burned their way into the hearts of His disciples, who were not able to understand what the Lord said about His death, burial, and resurrection.

Moreover, the tenderest feelings of which our

Acts 16:32, 33: "And they spake unto him [the jailer] the word of the Lord, and to all that were in his house. And he took them the same hour of the night, and washed their stripes; and was baptized, he and all his *straightway*."

[1]Luke 22:19: "And he took bread, and gave thanks, and brake it, and gave unto them, saying, This is my body which is given for you: this do in remembrance of me."

[2]1 Cor. 11:23: "For I have received of the Lord that which also I delivered unto you, That the Lord Jesus, the same night in which he was betrayed, took bread."

48

natures are capable under the inspiration of the Holy Spirit are awakened when we meditate on the death of our Lord, partaking of the elements which our Lord himself chose to symbolize His broken body and shed blood.

2. WE ARE INSTRUCTED TO SEARCH OUR HEARTS DILIGENTLY AND EXAMINE OURSELVES CAREFULLY before coming to this holy ordinance, and to approach it with reverence and understanding (1 Cor. 11:27-32).*

3. OUR LORD COMMANDED HIS DISCIPLES TO OBSERVE IT. "Take, eat. . . . Drink ye all of it" (Matt. 26:26,27; the Greek reads: "All of you drink of it"). "This do . . . " (1 Cor. 11:24). We are not given any option in regard to observing this memorial of His death. Our Lord himself commands it, and we

---

*1 Cor. 11:27-29: "Wherefore whosoever shall eat the bread or drink the cup of the Lord in an unworthy manner, shall be guilty of the body and the blood of the Lord. But let a man prove himself, and so let him eat of the bread, and drink of the cup. For he that eateth and drinketh, eateth and drinketh judgment unto himself, if he discern not the body" (ASV).

"In an unworthy manner"—without proper regard for the significance and sacredness of the ordinance—in a disorderly, irregular way. "Guilty of the body and the blood of the Lord"—guilty of partaking of the emblems of our Lord's body and blood in an unholy, unworthy, sacrilegious manner; "casting contempt on His body and blood" (Worrell, p.246, footnote).

"Prove himself"—make a careful scrutiny of himself and of his conduct in the light of the Word. "So . . . "—after squaring himself with the Word.

"Eateth and drinketh judgment unto himself." The King James Version has "damnation." This word is too strong, according to the Greek. Not eternal "damnation," but a judgment from God to chasten the believer, that he "may not be condemned with the world" (see vv. 31,32).

must answer to Him if we refuse to obey. It is a *perpetual* ordinance, to be *frequently observed,* for Paul says: "As often as ye eat this bread, and drink this cup, ye do show the Lord's death till he come" (1 Cor. 11:26).

4. THE HOLY SUPPER LOOKS FORWARD TO THAT DAY WHEN OUR LORD SHALL RETURN, and drink of the fruit of the vine "new" with His own in His Father's kingdom (Matt. 26:29). Hence, it keeps us "looking for that blessed hope, and the glorious appearing of the great God and our Saviour Jesus Christ" (Titus 2:13).

5. "THE CUP," "THE FRUIT OF THE VINE," representing the blood of Jesus, is a symbol of the sealing of the new covenant with His lifeblood. As our Lord himself declared: "This is my blood of the new testament, which is shed for many for the remission of sins" (Matt. 26:28). The Revised Standard Version gives us "covenant" instead of "testament." It is not the book we call the New Testament, but the new covenant foretold in Jeremiah 31:31-34.

Weymouth's free rendering makes this clearer: "This is my blood, poured out for many for the forgiveness of sins"—the blood which ratifies the covenant. In Luke 22:20, the words are given in a little different order: "This cup is the new testament in my blood, which is shed for you." Weymouth renders these words: "This cup . . . is the new Covenant ratified by my blood which is to be poured out on your behalf."

In Hebrews 9:16-18, this covenant is considered as a "will and testament," and this is the primary meaning of the Greek word translated "covenant." The writer holds that a will is of no effect as long as the "testator" lives. To make the will of force the testator must die. The blood of Jesus is proof of His death. He sealed the covenant with His lifeblood, and thus ratified it and made it effectual and operative. This is a thrilling thought for us who are heirs of God, and joint-heirs with Christ (Rom. 8:17).

6. THE ORDINANCE OF BAPTISM SYMBOLIZES CHRIST'S DEATH for us and our death to the world and union with Him (Rom. 6:3-5; Col. 2:12). *The Lord's Supper signifies the death of our Lord on our behalf* as our Paschal Lamb, sacrificed to deliver us from sin and death—in the purpose of God, "slain from the foundation of the world" (Rev. 13:8). Baptism signifies our entering into Christ and our new life in union with Him through regeneration. The Lord's Supper signifies Christ's entering into us, procuring our sanctification, sustaining, strengthening, and renewing. As baptism is associated with the new birth, we need to be baptized once, but one who is born needs constant nourishment, and for that reason we observe the Lord's Supper frequently.

For this reason bread, "the staff of life," is the most appropriate symbol that could be chosen. And this accords with the words of Jesus:

"I am that bread of life. Your fathers did eat manna in the wilderness, and are dead. This is the bread which cometh down from heaven, that a man may eat thereof, and not die. I am the living bread which came down from heaven: if any man eat of this bread, he shall live forever: and the bread that I will give is

51

my flesh, which I will give for the life of the world"
(John 6:48-51).

"Verily, verily, I say unto you, Except ye eat the flesh of the Son of man, and drink his blood, ye have no life in you. Whoso eateth my flesh, and drinketh my blood, hath eternal life; and I will raise him up at the last day. For my flesh is meat indeed, and my blood is drink indeed. He that eateth my flesh, and drinketh my blood, dwelleth in me, and I in him. As the living Father hath sent me, and I live by the Father; so he that eateth me, even he shall live by me. This is that bread which came down from heaven: not as your fathers did eat manna, and are dead: he that eateth of this bread shall live for ever" (John 6:53-58). (Read also verses 32-35.)

7. THE LORD'S SUPPER IS A HEALING ORDINANCE. If you are sick or afflicted in your body and can discern the healing virtue in the body of our Lord, typified by the bread, you may receive healing and strength for your body as well as for your spiritual nature.*

---

*1 Cor. 11:30-32: "For this cause many are weak and sickly among you, and many sleep. For if we would judge ourselves, we should not be judged. But when we are judged, we are chastened of the Lord, that we should not be condemned with the world."

"For this cause"—for failure to discern the true significance of the sacrifice of the body of Christ, symbolized by the bread. His body for our bodies, as the body of the paschal lamb was to be roasted and eaten—to give strength, health, and healing for the bodies of the Israelites to prepare them for the Exodus. The blood was to protect them from "the destroyer." Read the whole account in Exodus 12. Worrell's note on this verse is illuminating: "*Many are weak and sick*; a failure to appreciate the full meaning of the ordinance, and to appropriate its meaning as symbolized in the bread and wine, left many of the Corinthian brethren out of vital touch with God for their bodies; hence their

8. It Is a Uniting Ordinance. The ordinance of baptism should bring us into a closer fellowship with Christ our Lord, and the Lord's Supper should bring us into fellowship, not only with Him, but also with one another, as a family of God, feasting together and partaking of one bread and one cup. "The cup of blessing which we bless, is it not the communion of the blood of Christ? The bread which we break, is it not the communion of the body of Christ? For we being many are *one* bread, and *one* body: for we are all partakers of that *one* bread" (1 Cor. 10:16, 17).

9. The Ordinances of the New Testament help us to sense the reality of spiritual things. They picture the most fundamental truths of the gospel before our eyes. In baptism we go into a watery grave and feel it surging about us, and ourselves sinking beneath it and rising above it; indicating our own death and resurrection, as well as Christ's.

The Lord's Supper speaks to our hearts, to our eyes, and to our touch and taste. John says: "That which was from the beginning, which we have heard, which we have seen with our eyes, which we have looked upon, and our hands have handled, of the Word of life" (1 John 1:1). So in the Lord's Supper we see the bread, indicating the body of our Lord, broken before our eyes; we take a morsel into our hands and then into our mouths; we see the fruit of the vine, typifying the blood of Jesus, poured forth before our eyes; we drink it, appropriate it. All this

---

weakness and sickness. *And not a few sleep*; sleep the sleep of death."

gives us a sense of reality, which perhaps we could acquire in no other way, and signifies how absolutely necessary it is for our souls and bodies to be sustained by the life-giving Christ, who died and lives again, delivering us from sin and healing our bodies.

The more we see in the ordinances, the more they mean to us and the larger the measure of blessing conveyed. May God give us grace ever to approach this holy ordinance with a feeling of reverence and awe and love such as we have never known before.

7

The Baptism in the Holy Ghost

Following Worrell's very correct rendering of the original in Acts 1:4,5, we read: "And, being assembled together with them, He commanded them not to depart from Jerusalem, but to wait for the promise of the Father, which, said He, 'Ye heard from Me; because John, indeed, immersed in water, but ye shall be immersed in the Holy Spirit, not many days hence.'" Note that it is not *a* promise, but *the* promise, the great mountain-peak promise which towers above all the rest of the Father's promises following the fulfillment of the promise of the Messiah. Our Saviour himself gave us the phrase. Let us try to formulate the Bible's teaching concerning this "promise of the Father" in such a simple way that none may fail to apprehend it.

1. IN THE OLD TESTAMENT THE HOLY SPIRIT IS REVEALED AS THE LIFE-GIVER (Gen. 1:2; cf. Rom. 8:2), and with this Spirit prophets, priests, and kings were anointed. The promise of the general effusion of the Spirit on all flesh referred to a later time—the time following the ascension of our Lord to appear in the upper sanctuary (heaven), and offer up himself, the full price of our redemption.*

---

*Heb. 9:11,12: "But Christ being come a high priest of good things to come, by a greater and more perfect tabernacle, not made with hands, that is to say, not of this building; neither by

These great promises for the future outpouring of the Spirit are found in Isaiah 32:15: "Until the Spirit be poured upon us from on high"; and 44:3: "For I will pour water [a symbol of the Spirit] upon him that is thirsty, and floods upon the dry ground: I will pour my Spirit upon thy seed, and my blessing upon thine offspring."

Then in Joel 2:28, 29 we have that great prediction which had its partial fulfillment at Pentecost (the former rain), and is now being fulfilled in a more general diffusion of the Spirit all over the world (the latter rain).[1] (See Joel 2:23 and James 5:7, 8.[2]) Notice that the promise is to pour the Spirit upon *all flesh.*

2. JOHN THE BAPTIST FORETOLD THE SACRIFICE OF CHRIST, calling Him "the Lamb of God, which taketh

---

the blood of goats and calves, but by his own blood he entered in once into the holy place, having obtained eternal redemption for us." (Compare this with John 7:39.)

[1]The apostle Peter declares that the outpouring of the Spirit at Pentecost was a fulfillment of the above prophecy, which in our times again is having a more general fulfillment.

Joel 2:28,29: "And it shall come to pass afterward, that I will pour out my Spirit on all flesh; and your sons and your daughters shall prophesy, your old men shall dream dreams, your young men shall see visions: and also upon the servants and upon the handmaids in those days will I pour out of my Spirit."

[2]Joel 2:23: "Be glad then, ye children of Zion, and rejoice in the Lord your God: for he hath given you the former rain moderately, and he will cause to come down for you the rain, the former rain, and the latter rain in the first month."

James 5:7,8: "Be patient therefore, brethren, unto the coming of the Lord. Behold, the husbandman waiteth for the precious fruit of the earth, and hath long patience for it, until he receive the early and latter rain. Be ye also patient; stablish your hearts: for the coming of the Lord draweth nigh."

away the sin of the world" (John 1:29). He predicted also the office of Christ as the One who should baptize in the Holy Spirit: "I, indeed, immerse you in water unto repentance, but He Who is coming after me is mightier than I, whose sandals I am not worthy to bear, He will immerse you in the Holy Spirit and fire" (Matt. 3:11, Worrell).

It is to this prediction that our Lord himself refers in the text first quoted in this chapter. By these texts, together with Acts 11:15,16,* we know that Jesus alone can baptize in the Holy Spirit. (Compare this with John 1:29-34; 7:37-39.)

3. JESUS HANDED DOWN THIS PROMISE FROM THE FATHER. John 14:15-17 says: "If ye love me, keep my commandments, and I will pray the Father, and he shall give you *another Comforter* [Advocate], that he may abide with you for ever; even the Spirit of truth; whom the world cannot receive, because it seeth him not, neither knoweth him: but ye know him; for he dwelleth with you, and shall be in you." And verse 26 reads: "But the Comforter [Advocate], which is the Holy Ghost, whom the Father will send in my name, he shall teach you all things, and bring all things to your remembrance, whatsoever I have said unto you."

4. SO IMPORTANT DID OUR LORD REGARD THE SPIRIT'S COMING INTO THE LIFE OF BELIEVERS that He said: "It is expedient for you that I go away: for if I

*Acts 11:15,16: "And, as I began to speak, the Holy Spirit fell on them, as on us at the beginning; and I remembered the word of the Lord, how He said, 'John, indeed, immersed in water, but ye shall be immersed in the Holy Spirit' " (Worrell).

go not away, the Comforter [Advocate] will not come unto you; but if I depart, I will send him unto you" (John 16:7). Many Christians speak lightly of the gift of the Holy Spirit. This is an insult to the Spirit, to Jesus (who gave His life to procure for us the right to have the Spirit abiding in us), and to the Father (who in Jesus' name vouchsafes to us this supreme Gift). Without the Spirit's aid we cannot live as we should or do what we ought.

5. PETER IDENTIFIES THE PROMISE OF THE SPIRIT, OR THE BAPTISM IN THE SPIRIT, WITH THE GIFT OF THE SPIRIT. Acts 2:38,39 says: "Repent, and be baptized . . . and ye shall receive the *gift* of the Holy Ghost. For *the promise* is unto you, and to your children, and to all that are afar off, even as many as the Lord our God shall call." In Acts 11:16, 17, the gift of the Spirit and the baptism in the Spirit are made identical.

6. PETER SAYS THAT THE PROMISE IS FOR ALL BELIEVERS, and not for the apostles or for the hundred and twenty alone. "Unto you" (those present) and "to your children" (those absent and those yet unborn). "To all that are afar off"—that includes us. Acts 10 and 11 show that the Gift is for the Gentiles as well as for Jews.

7. PAUL TWICE REFERS TO THE GIFT OF THE SPIRIT AS A SEAL OR SEALING. Eph. 1:13 says: "In whom [in Christ] also, after that ye believed, ye were *sealed* with that Holy Spirit of promise"; or, to use our English idiom instead of the Hebrew, *the promised Holy Spirit*. Second Cor. 1:21,22 reads: "Now he which stablisheth us with you in Christ, and hath anointed us, is God; who hath also *sealed*

us, and given the *earnest* of the Spirit in our hearts."
The Christian's anointing and enduement with the
Spirit may be seen upon his countenance, observed
in his acts, heard in his voice, and felt in his
presence. The seal is upon his body, soul, and spirit.

8. THE GIFT OF THE SPIRIT IS AN EARNEST OR PLEDGE
OF OUR FULL INHERITANCE IN CHRIST. See the texts
cited under the last proposition. The gift of the
Spirit is proof positive that we are accepted in the
Beloved, and that we are joint-heirs with Him. (See
also Rom. 8:16,17.)

9. WITH THE BAPTISM COMES POWER FOR SERVICE.
The Holy Spirit is not given to believers as a spiritual
luxury for their personal satisfaction and enjoyment,
but as an enduement of power to fit them for bearing
effective witness to the great soul-saving truths of
the gospel. This was clearly stated by the Lord
himself, as He talked with His disciples after the
Resurrection: "And [He] said unto them, Thus it is
written, and thus it behooved Christ to suffer, and to
rise from the dead the third day: and that repentance
and remission of sins should be preached in his name
among all nations, beginning at Jerusalem. And ye
are witnesses of these things. And, behold, I send *the
promise of my Father* upon you: but *tarry ye* in the
city of Jerusalem, until ye be *endued*[1] *with power
from on high*" (Luke 24:46-49).[2]

---

[1]*Endue* is a Greek word in English letters. It means to clothe,
to put on (a garment or robe), to robe.
[2]John 7:37-39: "Now, on the last day, the great day of the
feast, Jesus stood, and cried, saying, "If anyone thirst, let him
come to Me and drink. He that believes on me, as the Scripture

Likewise in Acts 1:8: "But ye shall *receive power,* after that the Holy Ghost is *come upon* you: and ye shall be witnesses unto me both in Jerusalem, and in all Judea, and in Samaria, and unto the uttermost part of the earth."

Peter and John were commanded by the Jewish high council not to speak or teach anymore in the name of Jesus. After being threatened and then released, they went to their own company, who "lifted up their voice to God with one accord" (in Pentecostal fashion) and prayed for courage to speak the word of God with boldness. "And when they had prayed, the place was shaken where they were assembled together; and they were all *filled with the Holy Ghost"*—filled anew—"and they spake the word of God *with boldness.* . . . And *with great power* gave the apostles witness of the resurrection of the Lord Jesus: and *great grace* was upon them all" (see Acts 4:18-33). In several other passages we read of the refilling of the Lord's messengers for special service.

---

said, from within him shall flow rivers of living water.' But this He spake concerning the Spirit, Whom those who believed on Him were about to receive; for the Spirit was not yet given, because Jesus was not yet glorified" (Worrell).

Isaiah prophesied: "The parched ground shall become a pool, and the thirsty land springs of water" (35:7). But this promise goes far beyond that wonderful prediction. Think of whole rivers of living (life-giving) water from the life of one man or woman who was dry as powder before the Spirit came in to abide!—Niles, Amazons, and Mississippis from one life "filled with all the fulness of God" (Eph. 3:19). The Book of Acts proves the truth of these words of Jesus. Look at Pentecost! Look at Samaria! In later history, think of Luther, Wesley, Spurgeon, Moody, and Finney.

The gospel is to be propagated by the power of the Holy Spirit, who alone can convict sinners (John 16:8), piercing their hearts, as He did at Pentecost (Acts 2:37). (Compare this with Zech. 4:6.)

10. WITH THE BAPTISM IN THE SPIRIT SPECIAL GIFTS OF THE SPIRIT ARE FREQUENTLY BESTOWED. At Pentecost (Acts 2:5-11) the gift of tongues was temporarily exercised. (See chapter 8, "The Evidence of the Baptism in the Holy Ghost," for an explanation of the difference between the evidence of tongues and the gift of tongues.) At Ephesus the twelve men whom Paul found there were filled with the Spirit and not only spoke with tongues, but also "prophesied" (Acts 19:1-7).

Nine special gifts or manifestations of the Spirit are described in 1 Cor. 12:1-31. In chapter 13 the superiority of holy, divine love—a fruit of the Spirit—is shown. In chapter 14, Paul gives some regulations concerning the exercise of the gifts of the Spirit. In Hebrews 2:3,4, he shows how these gifts were used for the spread of the gospel: "How shall we escape, if we neglect so great salvation; which at the first began to be spoken by the Lord, and was confirmed unto us by them that heard him; God also bearing them witness, both with *signs and wonders, and with divers miracles, and gifts of the Holy Ghost,* according to his own will?"

This accords exactly with the record in Mark 16:20: "And they went forth, and preached every where, the Lord working with them, and *confirming the word with signs following.*" The whole Book of Acts is a commentary on this truth.

11. FOLLOWING THE BAPTISM IN THE SPIRIT, THE FRUIT OF THE SPIRIT naturally spring forth. In Galatians 5:22,23, Paul names the component parts of a cluster of precious fruit: "The fruit of the Spirit is love, joy, peace, long-suffering, gentleness, goodness, faith, meekness, temperance [self-control, continence]." It seems easier for us to speak of this composite fruit as separate fruits of the Spirit. In the regenerate life "the flowers of grace" may appear. How wonderful to observe the abundant luscious fruit in the lives of Spirit-filled Christians in whom the Spirit is reproducing the life and traits of Jesus Christ! (See 2 Cor. 3:18.)

In 1 Corinthians 13, the vast superiority of holy, divine love shines out above tongues, knowledge, faith, prophecy, and other gifts of the Spirit. These gifts may all become unnecessary and therefore cease "when that which is perfect is come," but such fruits as faith, joy, and love will abide forever, and the most beautiful and wonderful of all is *love*.

12. NUMEROUS NAMES ARE GIVEN IN THE SCRIPTURES TO THE HOLY SPIRIT, fitting the various relations, offices, and ministries which He fulfills. He is the Spirit of God (Eph. 4:30), the Spirit of Christ (Rom. 8:9), the Spirit of Truth (John 14:17), another Advocate or Paraclete (John 14:16). He is our Guide (John 16:13), our Teacher (John 14:26), our Reminder (John 14:26), our Helper (Rom. 8:26), our Revealer (1 Cor. 2:10), our Transformer (2 Cor. 3:18).

In the Authorized Version, if no mistake has been made in the count, the name *Holy Ghost* occurs 87 times in the New Testament. Four times the same

Greek words are translated "Holy Spirit" (Luke 11:13; Eph. 1:13; 4:30; 1 Thess. 4:8). Where the word translated "ghost" is not qualified by the word *holy* and yet refers to the divine Spirit, it is always translated "Spirit" in this version. In Acts 2:4, we have this word translated both ways: "They were all filled with the Holy Ghost [*pneuma*], and began to speak with other tongues, as the Spirit [*pneuma*] gave them utterance." In most later translations the word is uniformly rendered "Spirit" and this is a decided gain. (This is so in these versions: American Standard Version, Worrell's, Moffatt's, Weymouth's, Bible Union, Critically Emphasized, Twentieth Century, Centenary, Riverside, Greek-English Interlinear, New Covenant, Syriac, and other translations.)

13. "HE WILL BAPTIZE YOU IN THE HOLY SPIRIT AND FIRE."* Both water and fire are symbols of the Holy Spirit, and set forth the office work from different aspects. The water purifies by washing away; the fire

---

*As there are many types of the Lord Christ, so there are a number of symbols of the Holy Spirit, such as wind, breath, water, and fire. We give below some illuminating comments:

Adam Clarke in his commentary says, "He [the Spirit] is represented here under the similitude of fire, because he was to illuminate and invigorate the soul, penetrate every part, and assimilate the whole to the image of the God of glory." (See Matt. 3:11.)

"John, also, by contrasting the baptism in water with that in the Holy Spirit and fire, showed the superiority of Christ's office work and power over his own. As spirit and fire are more powerful, penetrating, and subtle than water, so Christ's work would be higher, more spiritual and profoundly searching than his, consuming the dross and producing a higher spiritual life, with all the attendant fruits and blessings" (Geo. W. Clark's commentary).

purifies by consuming and refining (Mal. 3:2,3).*
Isaiah was both purified and "fired for service" by the
"live coal" taken from the altar and laid on his mouth
(Isa. 6:6, 7). As fire coming into cold black iron can
make it red, then pink, then white and glistening; so
the Holy Spirit in the heart of the believer can soften
and melt him and warm his cold nature, illuminating
and inspiring him, and can make him, like John, "a
burning and a shining light" (John 5:35).

John shone because he was *"on fire,"* and so were

---

*The Holy Spirit—"The mightiest power in the universe for
renewing the heart and bringing in the kingdom of God. It would
be as easy to bring springtime without the sun as the kingdom of
God without the Holy Spirit. *And with fire.* The symbol of the
Holy Spirit. The sun is fire, the source of all light and heat,
purifying, health-giving, the source of beauty, comfort, life,
fruitfulness and all cheer and power. The fire was visibly
manifested on the Day of Pentecost, as a symbol of the perpetual
but invisible operation of the Holy Spirit on the hearts of men"
(Peloubet's *Commentary on Matthew*).

A. Maclaren: "The fire of God's Spirit is not a wrathful energy,
working pain and death, but a merciful omnipotence, bringing
light, and joy, and peace. The Spirit which is fire is a Spirit which
giveth life . . . . Christ comes to kindle in men's souls a blaze of
enthusiastic Divine love, such as the world never saw, and to set
them aflame with fervent earnestness, which shall melt all the
icy hardness of heart, and turn cold self-regard into self-
forgetting consecration" (*Sermon Bible*).

In his *Expositions of Holy Scriptures* the same writer says:
"Here is the power that produces that inner fervor without
which virtue is a name and religion a yoke. Here is the contrast,
not only to John's baptism, but to all worldly religion, to all
formalism, and decent deadness of external propriety. Here is
the consecration of enthusiasm—not a lurid, sullen heat of
ignorant fanaticism, but a living glow of an enkindled nature,
which flames because kindled by the inextinguishable blaze of
His love who gave himself for us, 'He shall baptize you in
fire.' "

the hundred and twenty at and after Pentecost. What would Pentecost be without the fire of the Holy Spirit?

14. THERE IS MUCH CONFUSION IN REGARD TO THE PERSONALITY OF THE HOLY SPIRIT.* In part this is due to lack of understanding in regard to the Biblical doctrine of the Holy Trinity, and in part to lack of consistency in the Authorized Version's renderings of texts referring to the Spirit. In some passages the masculine pronouns are used (John 14; 15; and 16), and in some texts we have neuter pronouns for the same Spirit (Rom. 8:16,26; and other passages).

This is to be accounted for by the fact that the Greek word *pneuma* (derived from *pneo*, to blow; both words being used in John 3:8), is a neuter noun. Originally it meant "breath" or "wind," and according to Greek grammar, the pronouns referring to this neuter noun had to be neuter. Hence, we have in Rom. 8:16 and 26: "the Spirit *itself.*" That is good Greek, but poor English. The American Standard

---

*In our Lord's farewell discourse, the Spirit is named the Paraclete, Advocate, Comforter—a masculine noun in the Greek—hence, we have no neuter pronouns here referring to Him. The Spirit is the other Advocate who is to abide with us forever. He has all the attributes and powers of divine personality: He speaks (Acts 1:16); works miracles (Acts 8:39); appoints missionaries (Acts 13:2); guides councils (Acts 15:28); directs His workers (Acts 8:29); commands and forbids (Acts 16:6,7); sets pastors over assemblies (Acts 20:28); witnesses (Rom. 8:16); aids us in prayer and intercedes (Rom. 8:26); foretells (Acts 20:22,23); and reveals to us the deep mysteries of God (1 Cor. 2:9-12). (See also the texts cited above.) Can any impersonal influence or power do such things? The question is too absurd to require an answer. The Book commonly called the Acts of the Apostles has been aptly called the Acts of the Holy Spirit.

Version, the Bible Union, Worrell's, Weymouth's, Centenary, and several other versions correctly translate the words, *"the Spirit Himself."* The Greeks knew that the pronouns had to agree in gender with the nouns to which they referred, hence they were not confused by these pronouns. In John 4:24, we have "God is a Spirit" (a neuter noun in Greek), but that does not justify us in referring to God as *"it"* or *"itself."**

---

*The Communion of the Spirit:
1. The Spirit of Life: Our Regeneration.
2. The Spirit of Holiness: Our Sanctification.
3. The Spirit of Glory: Our Transfiguration.
   —A. J. Gordon, *The Ministry of the Spirit* (Minneapolis: Bethany Fellowship, 1964).

8

The Evidence of the Baptism in the Holy Ghost

Notice it is not "The Baptism *of* the Holy Spirit," for that would make the Holy Spirit the agent; but John said, "He [Christ] shall baptize you *in* the Holy Spirit," as the Greek reads. The Holy Spirit is the element into which we are baptized.*

1. MANY BELIEVERS HAVE MIGHTY ANOINTINGS WITH THE HOLY SPIRIT WHO HAVE NOT RECEIVED THE FULLNESS OF THE BAPTISM.

In John 20:22, we read of the risen Christ: "And when he had said this, he breathed on them, and saith unto them, *Receive ye the Holy Ghost.*" It is certain that they received some very special enduement of the Holy Spirit; but this was not the

---

*As baptism in water is the immersion of the believer and the giving of the Spirit to believers is referred to under this figure, to be consistent we should avoid the phrases "baptism of or with the Holy Spirit." It is contradictory to say immersion with water or sprinkle in water. The Authorized Version was made by Episcopal clergymen who practiced sprinkling for baptism, hence we have "baptize with water," and "baptize with the Holy Ghost." The American Standard Version correctly translates the Greek in Acts 1:5: "Ye shall be baptized in the Holy Spirit." (Likewise the Centenary translation, the American translation, and the Concordant Version.) The Bible Union Version reads: "Ye shall be baptized [immersed] in the Holy Spirit." Worrell's translation says: "Ye shall be immersed in the Holy Spirit." Rotherham's Emphasized New Testament reads: "Ye in the Holy Spirit shall be immersed."

baptism in the Holy Spirit, for in the last visit of our Lord with the eleven He commanded them to tarry in Jerusalem and wait for the promise of the Father, saying, "Ye shall be baptized [in] the Holy Ghost not many days hence" (Acts 1:4, 5). If the disciples had been baptized in the Holy Spirit before this, our Lord would not have commanded them to wait for this promised Gift.

You may heat water to one hundred fifty degrees, then one hundred seventy-five, then two hundred, then to two hundred ten, but still it does not boil; but if it reaches two hundred twelve, it will boil. So you may be anointed with the Spirit almost to the fullness, but until there is actual fullness you do not have the baptism in the Holy Spirit.

2. THE BAPTISM IN THE HOLY SPIRIT IS NOT TO BE CONFUSED WITH SANCTIFICATION, AS IT IS BY MANY.

For in John 15:3, we read: "Now are ye clean through the word which I have spoken unto you." The baptism in the Holy Spirit presupposes that the believer is clean in the sight of God, and sanctification differs from the baptism in the Holy Spirit as the cleansing of the vessel differs from the filling of the same. At the baptism in the Holy Spirit we are filled to overflowing with the divine Presence.

3. SO DEFINITE AND SO WONDERFUL AN EXPERIENCE AS THE BAPTISM IN THE HOLY SPIRIT IS ACCOMPANIED WITH SUPERNATURAL EVIDENCE NOW AS IT WAS IN NEW TESTAMENT TIMES.

As our doctrinal statement declares, the baptism in the Spirit "is witnessed by the initial physical sign of speaking with other tongues as the Spirit of

God gives them utterance (Acts 2:4)." The mere experience of exuberant joy and abandonment to the will of God is not sufficient evidence, for these things may be experienced frequently before we receive the Baptism.

But when the Holy Spirit comes in His fullness to abide in the believer (John 14:16, 17), He takes possession of the spirit, soul, and body, which are then completely subjected to His will and power, and He uses the tongue in a supernatural way. This evidence is usually very convincing to believers and unbelievers alike who are present when one is baptized in the Holy Spirit. But, whether or not it is accepted by all who are present as full evidence, to the one who actually receives the Spirit, the speaking in tongues is an incontrovertible evidence, for *he knows that his vocal organs are under the control of the Spirit.*

4. WHEN PETER PREACHED AT THE HOUSE OF CORNELIUS THE HOLY SPIRIT FELL UPON ALL THAT HEARD THE WORD.

The Christian Jews who were present had to admit, though reluctantly, that on the Gentiles also was poured out the Holy Spirit, *"for they heard them speak with tongues and magnify God"* (Acts 10:46). To Peter and the rest of the Jewish Christians who were present, this was all-sufficient evidence that God had given these Gentiles the same gift that He had bestowed upon the hundred and twenty at the beginning. The brethren at Jerusalem called Peter to account for preaching to the Gentiles, but they acquiesced when Peter said, "Then remembered I the word of the Lord, how He said, John indeed baptized in water, but ye shall be baptized in the Holy Spirit'' (author's translation from the Greek, Acts 11:16).

5. WHEN PAUL CAME TO EPHESUS AND MET CERTAIN DISCIPLES, HE ASKED THEM, "HAVE YE RECEIVED THE HOLY GHOST SINCE YE BELIEVED?''

His question implied that some believed without receiving the Holy Spirit, and also that the reception of the Holy Spirit was so wonderful and was accompanied with such evidence that the recipients were able to answer the question definitely. The answer indicated that they were in the dark in regard to the baptism in the Holy Spirit, as many Christians are today. And after Paul baptized them in water and laid hands on them, the Holy Spirit came on them and *they spoke with tongues and prophesied* (Acts 19:1-7).

Suppose somebody had come along shortly after this and asked these twelve men the same question, do you suppose they would have been confused and unable to answer it? If they had been asked how they knew they had received the Holy Spirit, would they not have answered, "We spoke with other tongues as the Spirit gave us utterance''?

6. IN THE GREAT REVIVAL IN SAMARIA, there is no mention of the believers speaking in other tongues, but *something so wonderful happened to them that Simon the sorcerer offered a considerable sum for the power of bestowing the Holy Spirit.* If there had been no more evidence than the feeling of joy, it is not likely that Simon would have offered money for this power rather than the gift of healing. Moreover, *they had "great joy" before they received the Spirit*

70

(Acts 8:8). Hence, we believe that the experience of the disciples at Samaria in receiving the Holy Spirit was the same as that of the disciples at Jerusalem and Ephesus.

7. IN ACTS 9:17, WE HAVE THE ACCOUNT OF PAUL receiving his sight and being filled with the Spirit when Ananias came and put his hands upon him saying, "Brother Saul, the Lord, even Jesus . . . hath sent me, that thou mightest receive thy sight, and *be filled with the Holy Ghost.*" There is no mention of Paul's speaking in an unknown tongue, or of any other manifestation, at that time, but in 1 Corinthians 14:18, Paul says: "I thank my God, *I speak with tongues more than ye all.*" It is reasonable to suppose, therefore, that he began to speak in unknown tongues when he was filled with the Holy Spirit.

8. IN HEBREWS 2:4, WE READ: "GOD ALSO BEARING THEM WITNESS, both with signs and wonders, and with divers miracles, and gifts of the Holy Ghost, according to his own will." In Mark 16:17, Jesus says: "They shall speak with new tongues."

We have no record of any disciples speaking with new tongues before the Day of Pentecost, but it is evident from 1 Corinthians 14 and other Scripture passages that speaking with tongues was a frequent manifestation among believers; so frequent, indeed, that it was necessary for Paul to limit its use (1 Cor. 14:27) in public meetings, as is now the case in some Pentecostal assemblies.

The writer preached for thirty-one years before hearing anyone speak in unknown tongues and never found it necessary to refer to this Scripture passage to limit the exercise of this gift.

Through misinformation about the people who are filled with the Spirit and speak with tongues, and through ignorance of the Scriptures on the subject, many Christians in our times are prejudiced against "tongues" and forbid the exercise of this wonderful gift of the Spirit, contrary to the specific command of Paul, "Forbid not to speak with tongues" (1 Cor. 14:39); "I would that ye all spake with tongues" (v. 5); "I thank my God, I speak with tongues more than ye all" (v. 18).*

The emphasis that we place upon the gift of the Spirit, upon the scriptural evidence of His coming in to abide, and upon the necessity of following our Lord's command to "tarry until," distinguishes us from other bodies of believers. We esteem this Gift so

---

*The first instance of speaking in tongues was in the Upper Room, where the hundred and twenty were tarrying for the baptism in the Spirit. They all spoke the same language and understood each other without any other tongues. The purpose of this manifestation of the Spirit was not to make the gospel intelligible to people of different languages. It was an evidence of the baptism in the Spirit. They were all filled with the Holy Spirit, and began to speak with other tongues, as the Spirit gave them utterance (Acts 2:4). Jesus had said, "They shall speak with new tongues" (Mark 16:17). They appear to have gone down among the multitudes immediately, and there was the first manifestation of the gift of tongues. In this instance, the languages were understood by the various groups surrounding different disciples. From 1 Corinthians, it is evident that the gift of tongues was exercised in assemblies where all understood each other in the vernacular, and that these messages in tongues required interpretation, or no one would understand what was said. Hence, the gift of interpretation (1 Cor. 12:10; 14:2-23).

highly that we are willing to suffer reproach and loss for the sake of the wonderful privilege of receiving the Holy Spirit in the way the hundred and twenty did at Pentecost.*

---

*The history of the Pentecostal outpouring of the Spirit in our day, as related in that fine book, *With Signs Following,* by Stanley H. Frodsham, former editor of the *Pentecostal Evangel,* will inspire you. And so will the *Pentecostal Evangel* (the official organ of the Assemblies of God, published weekly), which is full of evidence of the mighty supernatural workings of God in these last days of this dispensation.

9

Sanctification

As a gifted writer has said, "If regeneration has to do with our nature, justification with our standing, and adoption with our position, then sanctification has to do with our character and conduct. In justification we are declared righteous in order that in sanctification we may become righteous. Justification is what God does for us, while sanctification is what God does in us. Justification puts us into a right relationship with God, while sanctification exhibits the fruit of that relationship—a life separated from a sinful world and dedicated to God."

1. SANCTIFICATION HAS A TWOFOLD MEANING: (1) SEPARATION FROM EVIL; (2) DEVOTION TO GOD.

First Thessalonians 4:3 says: "For this is the will of God, even your sanctification, that ye should abstain from fornication." (See also 2 Chron. 29:5, 15-18; 2 Tim. 2:21; Ex. 19:20-22.) In sanctification we are to cleanse ourselves from all filthiness of the flesh and spirit and at the same time perfect holiness in the fear of God (2 Cor. 7:1). But it is not enough to be separated from evil, the person or thing sanctified must be devoted to the use and service of God. Thus we read of sanctifying a house to be holy unto the Lord; part of a field to be God's possession. The first-born children were to be sanctified unto the Lord; and even Jesus himself was set apart ("sanctified") by the Father to carry out His will in the world. (See Lev. 27:14-16; Num. 8:17; John 10:36.)

2. IN ONE ASPECT SANCTIFICATION IS AN INSTANTANEOUS WORK.

"And such were some of you: but ye are washed, but ye are sanctified, but ye are justified in the name of the Lord Jesus, and by the Spirit of our God" (1 Cor. 6:11). "We are sanctified through the offering of the body of Jesus Christ once for all. . . . For by one offering he hath perfected for ever them that are sanctified" (Heb. 10:10, 14).*

When we believe on the Lord Jesus Christ and accept Him as our Saviour, we are justified by faith in Him and stand before God without any condemnation on our souls; we are regenerated, that is, born again through the operation of the Holy Spirit and the Word of God, and have become new creatures. We are also separated from sin and cleansed and purged by the blood of Jesus (1 John 1:7), and by our own will we set ourselves apart to the service of God, and Christ is now our "wisdom, and righteousness, and sanctification, and redemption" (1 Cor. 1:30). For this reason, all believers are designated "saints" in the New Testament, and Paul addresses the Corinthian believers (who were far from perfect) as "sanctified" (1 Cor. 1:2).

3. IN ANOTHER SENSE, SANCTIFICATION IS A PROGRESSIVE WORK.

---

*Heb. 9:13,14: "For if the blood of bulls and of goats, and the ashes of a heifer sprinkling the unclean, sanctifieth to the purifying of the flesh; how much more shall the blood of Christ, who through the eternal Spirit offered himself without spot to God, purge your conscience from dead works to serve the living God?"

It is carried on by the Lord Jesus Christ himself through the power of the Holy Spirit, until we attain a perfect likeness to himself. When we believe, the holiness of the Lord Jesus Christ is imputed to us, and before God we stand "complete in him" (Col. 2:10; cf 1:28), with His full righteousness placed to our credit. But it is another thing to have His holiness made actual in our lives.

This may be a long process and may require many experiences, including many chastenings of the Lord. In Heb. 12:10, we are distinctly told that God chastens us for the specific purpose that we may be *partakers of His holiness.* * Peter exhorts us to "grow in grace, and in the knowledge of our Lord and Saviour, Jesus Christ" (2 Peter 3:18). In 2 Cor. 3:18 we have a very illuminating text showing how Christ operates in us through the Holy Spirit to transform us by degrees into His own glorious image. In 1 Thess. 5:23, 24, Paul prays for these Thessalonian Christians: "The very God of peace sanctify you wholly; and I pray God your whole spirit and soul and body be preserved blameless unto the coming of our Lord Jesus Christ. Faithful is he that calleth you, who also will do it."

4. BOTH DIVINE AND HUMAN AGENCIES AND MEANS ARE USED TO SECURE SANCTIFICATION.

"And the very God of peace sanctify you wholly" (1 Thess. 5:23). Jesus says to His Father, "Sanctify them through thy truth" (John 17:17). God "[purifies our heart] by faith" (Acts 15:19).

---

*Heb. 12:10: "For they verily for a few days chastened us after their own pleasure; but he for our profit, that we might be partakers of his holiness." (See also Rom. 8:29.)

Christ is made unto us "sanctification" (1 Cor. 1:30), and by the offering of himself sanctifies the believers once for all (Heb. 10:10). "Christ . . . loved the church, and gave himself for it; that he might sanctify . . . it" (Eph. 5:25,26).

Our sanctification is not wrought out in us without the work of the Holy Spirit. First Peter 1:2 says: "Elect according to the foreknowledge of God the Father, through sanctification of the Spirit." The Holy Spirit comes in to make us partakers of the holiness of God. By showing us the truth as it is in the Word of God, and clarifying our vision to see Jesus, the Holy Spirit fires us with a longing to be like Him.

5. OUR OWN EFFORTS AND FULL COOPERATION WITH THE TRIUNE GOD ARE NECESSARY TO SECURE OUR ENTIRE SANCTIFICATION.

We are sanctified by faith in Christ. (See Acts 26:18.) We are to "cleanse ourselves from all filthiness of the flesh and spirit, perfecting holiness in the fear of God" (2 Cor. 7:1). John says: "Beloved, now are we the sons of God, and it doth not yet appear what we shall be: but we know that, when he shall appear, we shall be like him; for we shall see him as he is. And every man that hath this hope in him *purifieth himself, even as he is pure*" (1 John 3:2, 3).

In Phil. 3:12-14, Paul asserts that he has not yet attained to absolute perfection and that he is striving to reach this goal to which he has been called by the Lord. He adds: "Brethren, I count not myself to have apprehended: but this one thing I do, forgetting those things which are behind, and reaching forth unto those things which are before, I press toward the mark for the prize of the high calling of God in Christ Jesus."

6. GOD HAS PROVIDED MEANS WHICH ARE IN OUR REACH TO ATTAIN ENTIRE SANCTIFICATION.*

"Sanctify them through thy truth: thy word is truth" (John 17:17). Prayerful study of the Scriptures and an attentive listening to the messages from the Word of God by anointed servants of the Lord are designed as means toward our sanctification. Eph. 4:11, 12, shows us that our Lord gave the Church apostles, prophets, evangelists, pastors, and teachers, for the specific purpose of perfecting the saints.

In Heb. 12:14, we are told to "follow . . . holiness [sanctification], without which no man shall see the Lord." In the same chapter, we are told that chastisements are given by a loving Father to produce in us the "peaceable fruit of righteousness." In

---

*Romans 8:13: "For if ye live after the flesh, ye shall die: but if ye through the Spirit do mortify the deeds of the body, ye shall live."

Col. 3:5-14: "Mortify therefore your members which are upon the earth; fornication, uncleanness, inordinate affection, evil concupiscence, and covetousness, which is idolatry: for which things' sake the wrath of God cometh on the children of disobedience: in the which ye also walked sometime, when ye lived in them. But now ye also put off all these; anger, wrath, malice, blasphemy, filthy communication out of your mouth. Lie not one to another, seeing that ye have put off the old man with his deeds; and have put on the new man, which is renewed in knowledge after the image of him that created him: where there is neither Greek nor Jew, circumcision nor uncircumcision, Barbarian, Scythian, bond nor free: but Christ is all, and in all. Put on therefore, as the elect of God, holy and beloved, bowels of mercies, kindness, humbleness of mind, meekness, long-suffering; forbearing one another, and forgiving one another, if any man have a quarrel against any: even as Christ forgave you, so also do ye. And above all these things put on charity, which is the bond of perfectness."

78

Romans 6 and 2 Corinthians 6, and in numerous other Scripture passages, the believer is exhorted to separate himself from every evil and to devote himself unreservedly to God and His service, and thus to co-operate with God in his own sanctification, that he may attain to the measure of the fullness of Christ (Eph. 4:13).*

---

*"The sanctified life comes upon a full surrender, and may be lived by faith as one reckons himself to be dead indeed unto sin and alive unto God through Jesus Christ our Lord (Rom. 6:11). I feel that the weakness in our movement, when it comes to preaching sanctification, is that the doctrine is taught so vaguely that many fail to get sight of something definite which they may have in their own lives. It seems to me that if we teach that positionally we were sanctified, and eventually we will be wholly sanctified in the glory world, people are likely to look upon sanctification as a rather vague process, whereas I believe the Bible does teach that sin shall not have dominion over us, and that it is our privilege every moment to live victoriously as we reckon ourselves dead indeed unto sin but alive unto God through Jesus Christ our Lord. While we know sanctification is progressive, I would like to see more emphasis put upon a present experience as we take our position in the Lord."—Ernest S. Williams (in a letter to the author).

10

The Church and Its Mission

It is important at the outset to stress the *Biblical* meaning of our word *church*. The reason is that in current usage there are two meanings which are absent in Scripture.

One of these is a reference to a church building, which is often simply called a church. In New Testament times there were no buildings designated as churches. Instead, Christians met in homes for prayer and worship. A second non-Biblical meaning is the application of the word to a denomination or sect in Christendom, such as the Roman Catholic Church, the United Methodist Church, or the Pentecostal Church.

1. THE NEW TESTAMENT MEANING OF THE WORD *CHURCH*.

The word which is usually translated *church* is the Greek *ekklesia*, from which are derived such English words as *ecclesiastical*. But the Greek word was not originally a "religious" one. It was a word common to Greek-speaking pagans and was the designation for the group of men who at times were called out of their homes or places of business to conduct civic business. In a general sense, it was also used for a gathering of people. This secular usage of the term is found in Acts 19:32, 39, 41.

The Greek *ekklesia* comes from two words, one meaning "out of" (*ek*) and the other "to call" (*kalein*). Therefore, the root meaning is "to call out of." The

Church, therefore, consists of people who have been "called out of" sin and the world and who have assembled for a common purpose.

It is generally agreed among Greek scholars that the best translation for this Greek word is *assembly*—so that the designation "Assembly of God" is most appropriate for the name of a local congregation.

2. THE BIBLICAL USAGE OF THE WORD *CHURCH*.

There are two distinct but ultimately inseparable meanings of this word as it applies to believers. It is used, first of all, as a designation for a local congregation (Romans 16:5; 1 Corinthians 1:2; Galatians 1:2; 1 Thessalonians 1:1). It sometimes occurs in the plural to indicate separate groups of believers (*e.g.*, Galatians 1:2).

The second meaning is that of the whole company of regenerate persons regardless of location or time. In this regard it always appears in the singular—the Church (Ephesians 1:22; 3:21; Hebrews 12:23)—and emphasizes the unity of Christians throughout the world.

3. DERIVATION OF THE ENGLISH WORD *CHURCH*.

The origin of this word is the Greek *kyriakos* which means "belonging to the Lord." It seems that the Scottish *kirk* and the German *kirche* came from this, and in turn our English word *church*. It emphasizes that the Church is not a human organization but is of divine origin and is the Lord's own possession. It is an adjective and occurs only in 1 Corinthians 11:29 and Revelation 1:10—the Lord's Supper and the Lord's Day. Neither of these is directly related to our concept of church or assembly, however.

4. THE ORIGIN OF THE CHURCH.

Biblical expressions such as "churches of Christ" and "church of God" indicate clearly that it is the Lord's church. As such, it is not a human organization. Jesus said: "Upon this rock I will build my church" (Matthew 16:18). He is not only the Founder, but He is also the continuing strength of the Church. These words of Jesus are in the future tense, for it was not until the Day of Pentecost (Acts 2) that the Church was actually founded. This special day occurs seven weeks after Easter, and the Church has traditionally regarded it as its "birthday." It was on that day, following Peter's preaching, that the Church was firmly established by the addition of three thousand converts to the company of believers (Acts 2:41).

5. THE MEMBERS OF THE CHURCH.

A distinction must be made between human requirements and divine requirements for membership in the Church. It is possible to be a member of a church or denomination without being a member of the Church of Jesus Christ. Only those who have been saved or born again of the Spirit of God are true members of His church (Acts 2:47, *NASB*—"And the Lord was adding to their number day by day those who were being saved"). A person does not need to "apply" for membership in the universal Church; he is automatically a member when he is saved. This in no way eliminates the desirability of a Christian uniting himself with a local congregation of believers, for the local assembly is really a concrete manifestation of the unity of all believers in the universal Church.

6. TERMS FOR INDIVIDUAL MEMBERS.

In addition to the word *church* (assembly), there are two other designations commonly used in the Epistles to describe Christian believers—*saints* (Romans 1:7; 2 Corinthians 1:1; Ephesians 1:1) and *brethren* (Romans 8:29; 16:23; 1 Corinthians 1:1; 5:11). *Saints* comes from the Greek word for "separated ones." It does not necessarily mean that those so designated are perfect, but rather that they as Christians have been separated from a life of sin and are now living their lives in relation to God. In this respect it is closely related to the root meaning of the word for assembly (*ekklesia*) which, as we have already noted, directs attention to the "called-out" nature of believers.

Brethren stresses that all Christians belong to one spiritual family, whose Father is God himself. This term implies that all are equal before God; for, as Paul tells us, all believers are heirs of God and joint-heirs with Christ (Romans 8:17). One becomes a member of God's family by means of the new birth (John 3:3, 5).

7. FIGURES OF SPEECH FOR THE UNIVERSAL CHURCH.

The grandeur of the universal Church is such that it is impossible to describe it adequately. But the apostle Paul and others, under the direction of the Holy Spirit, help us to understand the nature of the Church more fully by employing three vivid figures of speech.

The Church is spoken of as the bride of Christ (2 Corinthians 11:2; Ephesians 5:25-27; Revelation 19:7; 22:17). This figure of speech speaks of the purity of the Church—something for which she must always strive. Jesus is the Bridegroom (Matthew 25:6; John 3:29). When He comes again, the Bride's time of preparation will be completed and she will be married to her heavenly Groom (Revelation 19:7-9; 21:2).

The Church is further presented in terms of a building, and specifically a temple (1 Corinthians 3:9, 16, 17; 2 Corinthians 6:16; Ephesians 2:20-22; 1 Timothy 3:15; 1 Peter 2:5; Revelation 21:3). In the Old Testament, the tabernacle and the temple were places where God manifested His presence in a special way. But God does not really dwell in material buildings as such (Acts 7:48, 49; 17:24, 25). His special presence is manifested today in a spiritual temple—the Church.

Each believer is a temple of the Holy Spirit (1 Corinthians 6:19), but the entire Church is also described as the temple of God (1 Corinthians 3:16, 17; 2 Corinthians 6:16-18). Christ is the chief cornerstone of this spiritual temple; the apostles and prophets are the foundation (Ephesians 2:20-22); and each believer is a "living stone" in the edifice (1 Peter 2:5). As a counterpart of the Old Testament tabernacle and temple, this spiritual building is a place where God is worshiped and served.

Finally, the Church is depicted in terms of a human body (Romans 12:4; 1 Corinthians 12:22-27; Ephesians 1:22,23; 3:6; 4:4,12,16; 5:23,30; Colossians

1:18,24; 2:19; 3:15). When all these passages are studied, the following important points emerge:

(1) Jesus Christ is the Head of the Church.

(2) Each believer is a member, or organ, of this Body.

(3) Individual believers cannot exist and act in isolation from other believers. There is an interdependence which is essential for survival.

(4) Just as Christ, in His earthly state, manifested himself to the world by means of His physical body, so today He accomplishes this by means of His spiritual body, the Church.

(5) Every believer has a vital function in the Church, even though it may seem insignificant.

(6) The individual members are to support and strengthen one another.

(7) Each member is directly related to the Head, the Lord Jesus Christ, who is the "nerve center" of the Body. Consequently, whatever touches one member of the Body affects not only other members but, most of all, the Head.

The Church as the body of Christ is therefore a living organism. It is more than just a collection of individual believers. It is the incorporation of each believer into the body of Christ (1 Corinthians 12:13), which makes him an integral part of that body.

8. The "Visible" and "Invisible" Church.

The Church is a spiritual fellowship comprising all who have been born again. Consequently, all true believers are united in the one flock of the Good Shepherd (John 10:16; 17:21-23). This spiritual, invisible bond finds concrete manifestation in the form of local congregations. Ideally, these should consist only of born-again believers. If this were absolutely true in every congregation, then it could be said that the "visible" church and the "invisible" Church are one and the same. But since there are some denominations and local churches which admit into membership people who are not truly saved, and since, further, it is possible for a person to *appear* to be a Christian without having a genuine conversion experience, we must conclude that the "visible" church cannot be equated with the "invisible" Church. Jesus' parable of the tares and the wheat is applicable at this point (Matthew 13:25-30, 36-43).

The Mission of the Church

God brought the Church into existence so it would be a means of bringing glory to His name. The apostle Paul tells us that the overall purpose of God's redeeming us is that we should be to the praise of His glory (Ephesians 1:6, 12, 14). The manner in which the Church glorifies God is three-directional: *outward*, in evangelism; *inward*, in edification of believers by one another; *upward*, in worship.

1. EVANGELIZATION.

This word literally means "a declaration or preaching of the gospel." The Greek word *evangelion*, from which we get our English "evangel," means "good news." "Evangel" and "gospel" are synonyms, so that when we speak of sharing the gospel with others we mean sharing the good news of Jesus Christ and His offer of salvation.

The field for evangelism is the whole world, as Jesus plainly commanded in Matthew 28:19,20, and Mark 16:15. The Church is under obligation to share the gospel with all men everywhere. This involves both home missions and foreign missions. Jesus stated that His followers were to be witnesses both near to home (Jerusalem, Judea, Samaria) and in more distant lands (uttermost parts of the earth), as we see in Acts 1:8.

It is important to note that this work of evangelism and missions can be carried out only by the power of the Holy Spirit. This is one very important function of the baptism in the Holy Spirit (Acts 1:8). God is glorified when new members are added to the body of Christ!

2. EDIFICATION.

The work of evangelism can be effective only when the body of Christ is healthy. Individual members of the Church have the responsibility to edify, or build up, one another. When they gather for worship, one purpose is that they might edify one another (1 Corinthians 14:26). Christians are enjoined to teach and admonish one another by preaching the Word, testifying,and singing (Ephesians 5:18,19; Colossians 3:16), and to attempt to help a sinning brother to see his sin so that he might repent of it (Galatians 6:1,2; James 5:19,20). There is the further responsibility of praying for one another, as Paul often did for the congregations to which he wrote (Ephesians 1:16-22).

3. WORSHIP.

The Church is the temple of God, and individual believers are priests who offer themselves and their praise as sacrifices to God (Romans 12:1; Hebrews 13:15). Therefore, when God's people assemble for worship, the primary focus must be on Him. When they come together to "minister to the Lord," then the Holy Spirit will be able to speak to them (Acts 13:2, 3).

Christians must take seriously the words of Scripture not to forsake the assembling of ourselves together (Hebrews 10:25). In the Old Testament, the seventh day of the week, the Sabbath, was reserved for the Lord. This principle of one day in seven is retained in the New Testament. It was the practice of the New Testament Church to come together on Sunday, the first day of the week, in commemoration of the resurrection of Jesus on that day (John 20:1; Acts 20:7; 1 Corinthians 16:2).

The worship which the Church renders to God must be "in spirit and in truth" (John 4:23,24); Philippians 3:3). It is a time when God's people, under the direction of the Holy Spirit and in accordance with God's Word, seek to glorify Him by means of song, prayer, and the ministry of the Word. A Spirit-filled congregation also experiences the gifts of the Spirit in its worship (1 Corinthians 14), by means of which God is glorified and the individual members are edified.

11

The Ministry

God wishes to accomplish His will for mankind through His church. It is, therefore, the responsibility of every born-again Christian to do what he can to fulfill the Lord's will in the three areas of evangelization, edification, and worship mentioned in chapter 10.

The Protestant Reformation recovered the great Biblical doctrine of the priesthood of all believers. This means that all Christians—both clergy and laymen—have direct access to God and may be used by Him for the accomplishment of His divine purposes.

Every Christian is a "minister," because the Greek word for this (*diakonos*) means "a servant, or one who ministers." The word today, however, is normally used to denote a person who is engaged full-time in the service of the Lord. It is in this "full-time" sense that the word *ministry* is used in this article.

Specific Ministries

Just as in every organization there must be a leadership, so it is with the Church. God has set up in the Church a number of specific offices. These are mentioned in Ephesians 4:11—apostles, prophets, evangelists, pastors, teachers. It will be profitable to look at each briefly.

1. APOSTLES AND PROPHETS.

Jesus initially called twelve men to be His close followers. They are designated "apostles"—a direct borrowing from the Greek word *apostolos,* which means "one who is sent." These men were given the responsibility of being the Lord's representatives in proclaiming the gospel. They are often referred to collectively as the twelve apostles.

The word *apostle* is also used in a wider sense in the New Testament, so that it includes people like Paul (Galatians 1:1), Barnabas (Acts 14:4,14), and James, the Lord's brother (Galatians 1:19). There is no one definition of the word *apostle* which clearly distinguishes such an individual from other ministers of the gospel. But it may be stated that an apostle is one who receives a direct commission from the Lord to perform a special task and who does an outstanding work for the kingdom of God. Even though the title may not be used today to designate such an individual, it is nevertheless true that there are those who have a very special, gifted ministry which they have received from God.

The word *prophet* comes from the Greek *prophetes,* which means "spokesman" or "someone who speaks on behalf of someone else." A prophet, therefore, is one who conveys God's message to men. Prophets are mentioned throughout the Old Testament and the New Testament. In the New Testament Church, however, the word is used specifically to designate those who exercise the gift of prophecy in corporate worship (1 Corinthians 14:29). At such times, the individual is prompted by the Holy Spirit to give a prophetic message. These messages do not necessarily have to do with predictions, for we are told that those who prophesy have the ministry of edifying (building up), exhorting, and comforting God's people (1 Corinthians 14:3). As with apostles, the title *prophet* is not usually applied to individuals even though such persons do indeed have a prophetic ministry. Women as well as men may prophesy (Acts 21:9; 1 Corinthians 11:5).

2. EVANGELISTS.

An evangelist is one who proclaims the gospel (from the Greek word *evangelion*—"good news"). Therefore, an evangelist is one who spreads the good news of Jesus Christ. As the apostle Paul expresses it, the gospel message centers on the death, burial, resurrection, and ascension of Jesus (1 Corinthians 15:1-7). The special function of the evangelist is to reach unsaved men with the message that Christ died for our sins and was raised for our justification (Romans 4:24, 25).

3. PASTORS.

The Greek word for *pastor* is the same as the word for *shepherd (poimen)*. The role of the pastor, therefore, is to see that the spiritual needs of his flock the congregation—are met (John 21:15-17, Acts 20:28).

Pastors are given two other designations in the New Testament—elders and bishops. When these leaders are called elders (*presbuteroi*, from which we get our English word *presbyters*), the emphasis is upon their spiritual maturity. These men are also referred to as bishops (*episkopoi*, which means *over-*

seers). But because this term now has a connotation quite different from that in the New Testament—namely, that a bishop is a minister who has oversight of *other* ministers—it is better to avoid calling a pastor a bishop.

The qualifications for a pastor or elder are clearly set forth in the Word of God: "A bishop then must be blameless, the husband of one wife, vigilant, sober, of good behavior, given to hospitality, apt to teach; not given to wine, no striker, not greedy of filthy lucre; but patient, not a brawler, not covetous; one that ruleth well his own house, having his children in subjection with all gravity; (for if a man know not how to rule his own house, how shall he take care of the church of God?) not a novice, lest being lifted up with pride he fall into the condemnation of the devil. Moreover he must have a good report of them which are without; lest he fall into reproach and the snare of the devil" (1 Timothy 3:2-7). There are similar qualifications listed in Titus 1:7-9.

4. TEACHERS.

Teachers constitute a distinct group of leaders in the Church (Acts 13:1; 1 Corinthians 12:28). It is their function to expound the Word of God to His people so that they may be firmly grounded in the faith. The ministry of teachers is directed to Christians.

5. DEACONS.

Deacons are not listed in Ephesians 4:9-11 as among the ministry gifts which Christ has bestowed upon the Church. Yet they too are ministers of the gospel inasmuch as the word *deacon* comes from the Greek *diakonos* which, as we have already seen, means "minister" or "servant." They are mentioned in conjunction with bishops in Philippians 1:1; and specific qualifications are given in 1 Timothy 3:8-13: "Likewise must the deacons be grave, not double-tongued, not given to much wine, not greedy of filthy lucre; holding the mystery of the faith in a pure conscience. And let these also first be proved; then let them use the office of a deacon, being found blameless. Even so must their wives be grave, not slanderers, sober, faithful in all things. Let the deacons be the husbands of one wife, ruling their children and their own houses well. For they that have used the office of a deacon well purchase to themselves a good degree, and great boldness in the faith which is in Christ Jesus."

According to Acts 6, the Early Church selected seven men who were to look after the temporal needs of God's people. These men are often referred to as deacons, although they are not specifically designated as such. Yet it is interesting to observe that the ministry of these men included other areas of service. At least two of them were also preachers—Stephen (Acts 6:8 to 8:3) and Philip (Acts 8:4-13; 21:8).

6. GENERAL OBSERVATIONS.

We have just noted that some ministers may have more than one type of ministry. For example, a pastor may have an evangelistic ministry (2 Timothy 4:5). He may also be gifted as a teacher (some people combine these two ministries into one).

Since every believer has the potential for exercising the gift of prophecy, then quite naturally a full-time minister of the gospel may also be a prophet. An examination of the gifts and offices mentioned in 1 Corinthians 12:28-31 further emphasizes that in the church of Jesus Christ there can be no rigid distinction between "clergy" and "laity," inasmuch as any believer may be selected by God for a specific ministry at a special time.

The Work of the Ministry

The overall purpose of the ministry is "for the perfecting of the saints, for the work of the ministry, for the edifying of the body of Christ" (Ephesians 4:12). This is accomplished first by leading unsaved men and women into a knowledge of Jesus Christ as their Saviour and Lord—which is the major function of the evangelist. When they become Christians, then pastors and teachers lead them into spiritual maturity. Thus, there is the fulfillment of the two goals of evangelization and edification.

Leadership in public worship is primarily the responsibility of the pastor. This type of worship will include the usual elements of worship, such as praise and singing, prayer, Scripture reading with comments (sermon), collections, and observance of the Lord's Supper (Matthew 18:19, 20; Acts 2:42-46; 1 Corinthians 16:1, 2; Ephesians 5:19, 20). In addition, the pastor will encourage the manifestation of the gifts of the Spirit in the services of worship (1 Corinthians 14:26).

12

Divine Healing

John Wesley, in his illuminating *Notes on the New Testament* (commenting on James 5:14,15), says: " 'Having anointed him with oil'—this single, conspicuous gift which Christ committed to His apostles (Mark 6:13) remained in the Church long after the other miraculous gifts were withdrawn. Indeed it seems to have been designed to remain always, and James directs the elders, who were the most, if not the only gifted men, to administer it. *This was the whole process of physic in the Christian Church, till it was lost by unbelief.... 'And the prayer offered in faith shall save the sick'*—from his sickness, and if any sin be the occasion of his sickness, it shall be forgiven him.''

In his *Journal,* John Wesley records no less than two hundred forty cases of divine healing in connection with his ministry. If this divine gift was lost through unbelief, it is reasonable to expect it to be restored through faith.

All through the centuries since the time of the apostles, there have been individuals who had faith in God for the healing of their bodies, and where *New Testament faith* has been found, *New Testament miracles* have been wrought in the name of Jesus Christ.

Near the end of the last century, there were a few shining lights who witnessed to the healing grace of our Lord in our times, but it was not till the mighty outpouring of the Holy Spirit in this century that the number of witnesses became large enough to attract the attention of the general public. During the past decade, divine healing has been brought into the limelight, and now thousands believe in it for every one who had the light fifty years ago.

Pentecostal people, one hundred percent strong, accept the doctrine of divine healing, and many of them have proved it in their own bodies. In addition, many who do not have the light on the baptism in the Holy Spirit in Pentecostal power, believe in the healing of the sick through the prayer of faith and will readily subscribe to the following propositions:

1. SICKNESS AND DEATH HAVE COME UPON THE HUMAN FAMILY BECAUSE OF SIN (Rom. 5:12).

2. THESE ARE NOT A BLESSING, BUT A CURSE permitted by God to fall upon man because of his sin and disobedience (Ex. 15:26;[1] Deut. 28:15-68).

3. NOT GOD, BUT THE DEVIL IS THE AUTHOR OF DISEASE AND DEATH. God is the Author and Giver of life and health, and Jesus came to *destroy the works of the devil*. This is shown in the Book of Job and in many other Scripture passages. (See Acts 10:38;[2] Luke 13:11-17; Heb. 2:14,15; 1 John 3:8.[3])

---

[1]Ex. 15:26: "If thou wilt diligently hearken to the voice of the Lord thy God, and wilt do that which is right in his sight, and wilt give ear to his commandments, and keep all his statutes, I will put none of these diseases upon thee, which I have brought upon the Egyptians: for I am the Lord that healeth thee."

[2]Acts 10:38: "How God anointed Jesus of Nazareth with the Holy Ghost and with power: who went about doing good, and healing all that were oppressed of the devil; for God was with him."

[3]Luke 13:11-17: "And, behold, there was a woman which had a

4. CHRIST WAS MADE A CURSE FOR US in order that we might go free from the curse of sin (Gal. 3:10-14).*

5. IN THE ATONEMENT FULL PROVISION IS MADE FOR OUR PHYSICAL HEALING, as well as for our deliverance

---

spirit of infirmity eighteen years, and was bowed together, and could in no wise lift up herself. And when Jesus saw her, he called her to him, and said unto her, Woman, thou art loosed from thine infirmity. And he laid his hands on her: and immediately she was made straight, and glorified God. And the ruler of the synagogue answered with indignation, because that Jesus had healed on the sabbath day, and said unto the people, There are six days in which men ought to work: in them therefore come and be healed, and not on the sabbath day. The Lord then answered him, and said, Thou hypocrite, doth not each one of you on the sabbath loose his ox or his ass from the stall, and lead him away to watering? And ought not this woman, being a daughter of Abraham, whom Satan hath bound, lo, these eighteen years, be loosed from this bond on the sabbath day? And when he had said these things, all his adversaries were ashamed: and all the people rejoiced for all the glorious things that were done by him."

Heb. 2:14,15: "Forasmuch then as the children are partakers of flesh and blood, he also himself likewise took part of the same; that through death he might destroy him that had the power of death, that is, the devil; and deliver them, who through fear of death were all their lifetime subject to bondage."

1 John 3:8: "He that committeth sin is of the devil; for the devil sinneth from the beginning. For this purpose the Son of God was manifested, that he might destroy the works of the devil."

*Gal. 3:10-14: "For as many as are of the works of the law are under the curse: for it is written, Cursed is every one that continueth not in all things which are written in the book of the law to do them. But that no man is justified by the law in the sight of God, it is evident: for, The just shall live by faith. And the law is not of faith: but, The man that doeth them shall live in them. Christ hath redeemed us from the curse of the law, being made a curse for us: for it is written, Cursed is every one that hangeth on a tree: that the blessing of Abraham might come on the Gentiles through Jesus Christ; that we might receive the promise of the Spirit through faith."

from the guilt, penalty, and power of sin (Isa. 53:4,5; Matt. 8:17; 1 Peter 2:24).[1]

6. THE BENEFITS OF HIS ATONEMENT CAN BE APPROPRIATED BY FAITH, AND IN NO OTHER WAY, and accrue to the believer only as his faith lays hold on them. The Lord asks us, "What wilt thou that I should do unto thee?" (Mark 10:51), and says, "According to your faith be it unto you" (Matt. 9:29).

7. DIVINE HEALING IS PART AND PARCEL OF THE GOSPEL (Luke 4:18, 19; Matt. 10:7, 8; Luke 10:9; Mark 16:15-20).[2]

8. IT IS GOD'S WILL TO HEAL ALL THE SICK, for Jesus and the apostles healed all that came to them for healing (Matt. 8:16; Acts 5:12-19).[3]

9. OUR LORD COMMITTED THIS HEALING MINISTRY FIRST TO THE TWELVE, THEN TO THE SEVENTY, AND THEN TO THE WHOLE CHURCH, AND FINALLY TO EACH

---

[1]Matt. 8:17: "That it might be fulfilled which was spoken by Isaiah the prophet, saying, Himself took our infirmities, and bare our sicknesses." (The King James Version does not properly translate the Hebrew text in Isaiah 53:4, but Matthew 8:17 gives the correct rendering.)

1 Peter 2:24: "Who his own self bare our sins in his own body on the tree, that we, being dead to sins, should live unto righteousness: by whose stripes ye were healed."

[2]Matt. 10:7,8: "And as ye go, preach, saying, The kingdom of heaven is at hand. Heal the sick, cleanse the lepers, raise the dead, cast out devils: freely ye have received, freely give."

Luke 10:9: "And heal the sick that are therein, and say unto them, The kingdom of God is come nigh unto you."

[3]Matt. 8:16: "When the even was come, they brought unto him many that were possessed with devils: and he cast out the spirits with his word, and healed all that were sick."

BELIEVER IN PARTICULAR. (See the texts cited under our seventh proposition. Read also John 14:12,13.)

10. THE LAST WORDS OF JESUS before He ascended on high, according to Mark 16:18, are a perpetual promise of this healing power: *"They [believers] shall lay hands on the sick, and they shall recover."* The final instructions given believers through James 5:14 directs them when sick to "call for the elders of the church," who are to anoint them and pray over them, and to this the great promise is added: "The prayer of faith shall save the sick, and the Lord shall raise him up."

11. NO MAN, CHURCH, KING, OR POTENTATE HAS ANY AUTHORITY TO COUNTERMAND THE LORD'S ORDERS.

12. CHRIST IS HEALING THE SICK IN OUR DAY. Wherever these directions are followed, the mighty works of our Lord are manifested.

"In that same hour he cured many of their infirmities and plagues, and of evil spirits; and unto many that were blind he gave sight. Then Jesus answering said unto them, Go your way, and tell John what ye have seen and heard; how that the blind see, the lame walk, the lepers are cleansed, the deaf hear, the dead are raised, to the poor the gospel is preached" (Luke 7:21, 22).

"Go . . . and tell John"—*every John.*

Acts 5:12,15: "And by the hands of the apostles were many signs and wonders wrought among the people . . . . insomuch that they brought forth the sick into the streets, and laid them on beds and couches, that at least the shadow of Peter passing by might overshadow some of them."

13

The Blessed Hope

"For the grace of God hath appeared, bringing salvation to all men, instructing us, to the intent that, denying ungodliness and worldly lusts, we should live soberly and righteously and godly in this present world; looking for the blessed hope and appearing of the glory of the great God and our Saviour Jesus Christ; who gave himself for us, that he might redeem us from all iniquity, and purify unto himself a people for his own possession, zealous of good works" (Titus 2:11-14, *ASV*).

Worrell, in his translation, calls this the "blissful hope." The word translated "blessed" is rendered "happy" in John 13:17 in the Authorized Version, but in the American Standard Version, from which most of the quotations in this chapter are taken, it is rendered "blessed." Let us see if we can discover what this hope is, and why it is designated blessed. It is the hope of the Rapture or the secret coming of the Lord for His own. This hope is founded on the plain, positive promises of Christ himself, often repeated and elucidated by the inspired writers of the Word of God. (See Luke 21:36; John 14:2, 3; 1 Thess. 4:13-17; Rom. 8:23, 24; 1 John 3:1-3.*)

---

*Luke 21:36: "Watch ye therefore, and pray always, that ye may be accounted worthy to escape all these things that shall come to pass, and to stand before the Son of man."

But why is this hope singled out and pronounced blessed? Because it means so much to the true child of God. Here we can do no more than indicate some of the blessings included in this hope.

1. THE RAPTURE WILL DELIVER US FROM THE GREAT TRIBULATION.

"Watch ye therefore, and pray always, that ye may be *accounted worthy to escape all these things that shall come to pass, and to stand before the Son of man*" (Luke 21:36). "Because thou didst keep

---

John 14:2, 3: "In my Father's house are many mansions: if it were not so, I would have told you. I go to prepare a place for you. And if I go and prepare a place for you, I will come again, and receive you unto myself; that where I am, there ye may be also."

1 Thess. 4:13-17: "But I would not have you to be ignorant, brethren, concerning them which are asleep, that ye sorrow not, even as others which have no hope. For if we believe that Jesus died and rose again, even so them also which sleep in Jesus will God bring with him. For this we say unto you by the word of the Lord, that we which are alive and remain unto the coming of the Lord shall not prevent them which are asleep. For the Lord himself shall descend from heaven with a shout, with the voice of the archangel, and with the trump of God: and the dead in Christ shall rise first: then we which are alive and remain shall be caught up together with them in the clouds, to meet the Lord in the air: and so shall we ever be with the Lord."

Rom. 8:23, 24: "And not only they, but ourselves also, which have the firstfruits of the Spirit, even we ourselves groan within ourselves, waiting for the adoption, to wit, the redemption of our body. For we are saved by hope: but hope that is seen is not hope: for what a man seeth, why doth he yet hope for?"

1 John 3:1-3: "Behold, what manner of love the Father hath bestowed upon us, that we should be called the sons of God: therefore the world knoweth us not, because it knew him not. Beloved, now are we the sons of God, and it doth not yet appear what we shall be: but we know that, when he shall appear, we shall be like him; for we shall see him as he is. And every man that hath this hope in him purifieth himself, even as he is pure."

the word of my patience, I also *will keep thee from the hour of trial,* that hour which is to come on the whole world, to try them that dwell upon the earth" (Rev. 3:10, *ASV*). The Greek reads, ". . . keep thee *out of* the hour of trial."

2. THE COMING OF CHRIST FOR HIS OWN IS OUR "IMMINENT AND BLESSED HOPE."

We are not looking for the Antichrist, or for the Tribulation. Our ears are attuned to hear the trumpet call of our Deliverer. Our eyes scan the skies, "looking for that blessed hope, and the glorious appearing of the great God and our Saviour Jesus Christ" (Titus 2:13). We are longing, looking, and *waiting* for God's Son from heaven (1 Thess. 1:10). "So Christ was once offered to bear the sins of many; and *unto them that look for him* shall he appear the second time without sin unto salvation" (Hebrews 9:28).

3. IN PREPARATION FOR THE RAPTURE, THE DEVIL AND HIS HOSTS WILL BE CAST DOWN FROM THE SKY.

The archangel Michael will clear the skies of all our spiritual foes, the devil and all his angels. As the Children of Israel were freed from the Egyptians and saw them no more after crossing the Red Sea, so at the Rapture, we will be forever done with the devil and all his cohorts, which now infest the air and afflict the children of men. Most graphically is this described in Revelation 12:7-12.* Practice on

---

*Rev. 12:7-12: "And there was war in heaven: Michael and his angels fought against the dragon; and the dragon fought and his angels, and prevailed not; neither was their place found any more in heaven. And the great dragon was cast out, that old serpent,

the "victory chorus," so that you may be ready to take your part when that day of triumph comes.

4. AT THE RAPTURE THE DEAD SAINTS WILL BE RAISED IN GLORY.

"For the Lord himself shall descend from heaven with a shout, with the voice of the archangel, and with the trump of God; and the dead in Christ shall rise first" (1 Thess. 4:16). "First"—that is before anything is done for the living saints. In 1 Corinthians 15:52, Paul says: "For the trumpet shall sound, and the dead shall be raised incorruptible." Of the resurrection body, he says in the same chapter: "It is sown in corruption: it is raised in incorruption: it is sown in dishonor; it is raised in glory: it is sown in weakness, it is raised in power: it is sown a natural body, it is raised a spiritual body" (vv. 42-44)—that is, a body adapted to live in a spiritual world.

5. AT THE RAPTURE, THE LIVING SAINTS WILL BE CHANGED.

"Behold, I tell you a mystery: We all shall not sleep

---

called the Devil, and Satan, which deceiveth the whole world: he was cast out into the earth, and his angels were cast out with him. And I heard a loud voice saying in heaven, Now is come salvation, and strength, and the kingdom of our God, and the power of his Christ: for the accuser of our brethren is cast down, which accused them before our God day and night. And they overcame him by the blood of the Lamb, and by the word of their testimony; and they loved not their lives unto the death. Therefore rejoice, ye heavens, and ye that dwell in them. Woe to the inhabiters of the earth and of the sea! for the devil is come down unto you, having great wrath, because he knoweth that he hath but a short time."

[die], but we shall all be *changed*, in a moment, in the twinkling of an eye, at the last trump: for the trumpet shall sound, and the dead shall be raised incorruptible, and we shall be *changed*" (1 Cor. 15:51,52, *ASV*). In Philippians 3:20,21, Paul throws more light on this change which we are to experience: "For our citizenship is in heaven; whence also we wait for a Saviour, the Lord Jesus Christ: who shall *fashion anew the body of our humiliation*, that it may be *conformed to the body of his glory*" (*ASV*). And John tells us: "We shall be *like him;* for we shall see him as he is" (1 John 3:2). This *transformation* in the bodies of the dead and the living saints at the coming of Christ is called by Paul "*the redemption of our body*" (Romans 8:23).

6. At the Rapture, the Living Saints Will Be Caught up Together With the Dead Saints, Who Are First Raised in Incorruption.

"Then [following the resurrection of the dead in Christ] we which are alive and remain [that are left] shall be caught up . . . in the clouds, to meet the Lord in the air" (1 Thess. 4:17). This is referred to as "our gathering together unto him" (2 Thess. 2:1). Blessed gathering! *Blessed hope!*

7. The Rapture Enables Both the Living and the Dead in Christ to Triumph Over Death and the Grave.

"But when this corruptible shall have put on incorruption, and this mortal shall have put on immortality, then shall come to pass the saying that is written [in Isaiah 25:8], *Death is swallowed up in victory*" (1 Cor. 15:54). This thought inspired Paul to write a stanza in triumph, imitating the wonderful words of Hosea 13:14:

Where, O death, is thy sting?
Where, O grave, is thy victory?
The sting of death is sin;
The power of sin is the law;
Thanks be to God, who giveth us the victory
Through our Lord Jesus Christ.

(1 Corinthians 15:55-57, author's translation from the Greek)

8. THE RAPTURE WILL LIFT THE SAINTS FOREVER ABOVE PAIN, SICKNESS, AND SORROW.

Read it for yourself in the soul-thrilling words of Holy Writ (Hosea 13:14; Rev. 7:16, 17; 14:13; 21:4). From a world of poverty and pain, of madness and misery, of sorrow and suffering, of war and woe, of weeping and wailing, of death and desolation, we will be snatched away into a land of eternal life and peace and joy and bliss, far removed from all the troubles of this sinful world. There "God shall wipe away all tears" (Rev. 7:17), and "sorrow and sighing shall flee away" (Isa. 35:10). What a change! *Blessed hope!*

9. AT THE RAPTURE THE SAINTS WILL BE REWARDED ACCORDING TO THEIR WORKS.

"Behold, I come quickly; and *my reward is with me*, to render to each man *according as his work is*" (Rev. 22:12, *ASV*). One good look at Him will a thousand sacrifices repay. His "well done" will requite all your labor. His "enter thou into the joy of thy Lord" will enrapture your heart.

Blessed hope! Anchor of sea-tossed mariners; guiding star of hope for way-worn pilgrims! May our tear-dimmed eyes ever behold this star of hope, till the "bright and morning star" appears, till the "daystar arises." "So shall we ever be with the Lord" (1 Thess. 4:17). "As for me, I will behold thy face in righteousness: I shall be satisfied, when I awake, with thy likeness" (Psalm 17:15). "In thy presence is fulness of joy; at thy right hand there are pleasures for evermore" (Psalm 16:11). *Blessed hope!*

14

The Millennial Reign of Christ

The word *millennium* is a Latin word, derived from *mille,* thousand, and *annum,* year. It means a thousand-year period of time in general, and in particular refers to the reign of Christ on earth, which will last for one thousand years. The great text on this theme is Revelation 20:1-10. In the first seven verses of this chapter the period of a thousand years is mentioned six times.

1. THERE ARE TWO GREAT SCHOOLS OF INTERPRETATION CONCERNING THE MILLENNIUM.

The first is *postmillennialism,* and the second is *premillennialism.* The postmillennialists hold that the Millennium will be produced by the preaching of the gospel and the forces now at work in the world, and that Christ will not come till after the Millennium, when He will appear to judge the living and the dead and to fix their eternal states. Until about 1900, this view was held by nearly all the orthodox churches. Such men as Charles H. Spurgeon, Dwight L. Moody, J. Wilbur Chapman, A. J. Gordon, and A. B. Simpson, and others who would not accept this teaching were considered peculiar and their teaching dangerous. Many so-called Modernists take this postmillennial view or else utterly deny the return of Christ.

The premillennial view (held by most Fundamentalists) maintains that man in this age, as in all ages, will prove a complete failure and that, instead of getting better, the world is ripening for judgment and is not going to drift gradually into, or evolve into, a Millennium. This view holds that there will be, and can be, no Millennium until Christ *personally appears with the holy angels and all the saints to execute judgment upon His enemies* (Jude 14,15),[1] and to destroy everything that offends, every vestige of the reign of Satan and the Antichrist (Matt. 13:41; Dan. 2:34, 35).[2] This is one of the cardinal doctrines of the Assemblies of God.

2. THE JEWS WILL BE REGATHERED TO PALESTINE (Ezek. 36:24-28).[3]

The temple in Jerusalem will be rebuilt, and Jeru-

---

[1]Jude 14, 15: "And Enoch also, the seventh from Adam, prophesied of these, saying, Behold, the Lord cometh with ten thousands of his saints, to execute judgment upon all, and to convince all that are ungodly among them of all their ungodly deeds which they have ungodly committed, and of all their hard speeches which ungodly sinners have spoken against him."

[2]Matt. 13:41: "The Son of man shall send forth his angels, and they shall gather out of his kingdom all things that offend, and them which do iniquity."

Dan. 2:34,35: "Thou sawest till that a stone was cut out without hands, which smote the image upon his feet that were of iron and clay, and brake them to pieces. Then was the iron, the clay, the brass, the silver, and the gold, broken to pieces together, and became like the chaff of the summer threshing-floors; and the wind carried them away, that no place was found for them: and the stone that smote the image became a great mountain, and filled the whole earth."

[3]Ezek. 36:24,28: "For I will take you from among the heathen, and gather you out of all countries, and will bring you into your own land. . . . And ye shall dwell in the land that I gave to your fathers; and ye shall be my people, and I will be your God."

Note: Most devout students of prophecy hold that the Jews

salem will be the center of our Lord's administration (Jer. 3:17; Micah 4:8).[1] The Lord will build again the *tabernacle of David*, which is fallen (Amos 9:11, 12; Acts 15:16, 17).[2]

3. DURING THE MILLENNIUM, OUR LORD WILL LIFT THE CURSE FROM MAN, AND FROM THE ANIMATE AND THE INANIMATE CREATION.

The whole earth will become exceedingly fertile

---

will return to Palestine in unbelief, as they are doing at this day; that the Antichrist will make a covenant with them, but later will break the covenant and will gather all nations together to destroy them completely; that when brought face to face with utter destruction and extinction, the Jews will realize their great national sin of unbelief and their spiteful rejection of Jesus the Christ, and will weep and wail in deepest penitence, and cry to God to send back His Son to be their Deliverer; and that they will welcome Him back as their Saviour and King. Many Scripture passages could be cited to support this view. Those who wish to go deeper into this subject will do well to read Blackstone's *Jesus Is Coming*, and other excellent books illuminating the prophetic pages of the Scriptures.

[1]Jer. 3:17: "At that time they shall call Jerusalem the throne of the Lord; and all the nations shall be gathered unto it, to the name of the Lord, to Jerusalem: neither shall they walk any more after the imagination of their evil heart."

Micah 4:8: "And thou, O tower of the flock, the stronghold of the daughter of Zion, unto thee it shall come, even the first dominion; the kingdom shall come to the daughter of Jerusalem."

[2]Amos 9:11,12: "In that day will I raise up the tabernacle of David that is fallen, and close up the breaches thereof; and I will raise up his ruins, and I will build it as in the days of old: that they may possess the remnant of Edom, and of all the heathen, which are called by my name, saith the Lord that doeth this."

Acts 15:16,17: "After this I will return, and will build again the tabernacle of David, which is fallen down; and I will build again the ruins thereof, and I will set it up: that the residue of men might seek after the Lord, and all the Gentiles, upon whom my name is called, saith the Lord, who doeth all these things."

and fruitful (Rom. 8:19-23; Ezek. 36:30,35; Isa. 35:1,2).[1]

4. DURING THE MILLENNIUM THE WORLD WILL ENJOY A THOUSAND YEARS OF PEACE UNDER THE PACIFIC REIGN OF THE PRINCE OF PEACE.

There will be no need of powerful standing armies and great navies, or military camps for training. Implements of destruction will be made into implements of agriculture (Hosea 2:18; Isaiah 2:4; Micah 4:3).[2]

---

[1]Rom. 8:19-23: "For the earnest expectation of the creature waiteth for the manifestation of the sons of God. For the creature was made subject to vanity, not willingly, but by reason of him who hath subjected the same in hope; because the creature itself also shall be delivered from the bondage of corruption into the glorious liberty of the children of God. For we know that the whole creation groaneth and travaileth in pain together until now. And not only they, but ourselves also, which have the firstfruits of the Spirit, even we ourselves groan within ourselves, waiting for the adoption, to wit, the redemption of our body."

Ezek. 36:30,35: "And I will multiply the fruit of the tree, and the increase of the field, that ye shall receive no more reproach of famine among the heathen . . . . And they shall say, This land that was desolate is become like the garden of Eden; and the waste and desolate and ruined cities are become fenced, and are inhabited."

Isa. 35:1,2: "The wilderness and the solitary place shall be glad for them; and the desert shall rejoice, and blossom as the rose. It shall blossom abundantly, and rejoice even with joy and singing: the glory of Lebanon shall be given unto it, the excellency of Carmel and Sharon; they shall see the glory of the Lord, and the excellency of our God."

[2]Hosea 2:18: "And in that day will I make a covenant for them with the beasts of the field, and with the fowls of heaven, and with the creeping things of the ground: and I will break the bow and the sword and the battle out of the earth, and will make them to lie down safely."

Isa. 2:4: "And he shall judge among the nations, and shall

5. DURING THIS GLORIOUS PERIOD THE TERM OF LIFE WILL BE GREATLY LENGTHENED.

Death will be the exception rather than the rule (Isaiah 65:20-23).[1] Satan will be bound and imprisoned—we'll have no tempter then (Rev. 20:1, 2).

6. THE HOLY SPIRIT WILL BE POURED OUT ON ALL FLESH (Joel 2:28,29).

A nation will be born in a day (Isa. 66:8), and the *Gentiles will come* to the brightness of Christ's glorious, righteous reign (Isaiah 55; 60).

7. ALL MANKIND—FROM THE YOUNGEST TO THE ELDEST—WILL KNOW THE LORD.

The whole earth will be filled with the glory of the Lord, and He will be King over all the earth (Zech. 14:9; Isaiah 2:2).[2]

---

rebuke many people: and they shall beat their swords into plowshares, and their spears into pruning hooks: nation shall not lift up sword against nation, neither shall they learn war any more."

Micah 4:3: "And he shall judge among many people, and rebuke strong nations afar off; and they shall beat their swords into plowshares, and their spears into pruning hooks: nation shall not lift up a sword against nation, neither shall they learn war any more."

[1]Isa. 65:20,23: "There shall be no more thence an infant of days, nor an old man that hath not filled his days: for the child shall die a hundred years old .... They shall not labor in vain, nor bring forth for trouble; for they are the seed of the blessed of the Lord, and their offspring with them."

[2]Zech. 14:9: "And the Lord shall be King over all the earth: in that day shall there be one Lord, and his name one."

Isa. 2:2: "And it shall come to pass in the last days, that the mountain of the Lord's house shall be established in the top of the mountains, and shall be exalted above the hills; and all nations shall flow unto it."

The Lord God of heaven has decreed it; Jesus taught it; the Bible predicted it; prophets foretold it; psalmists chanted it; angels announced it; the Transfiguration prefigured it; the apostles preached it; and the Cross assures it.

O glorious day! for which millions of hearts have longed; for which the oppressed, the sorrowing, the suffering of the earth have cried; for which the animal creation in its suffering groans; for which all nature waits—the day of the personal, glorious reign of our Lord and Saviour Jesus Christ with His saints in robes of white and all His holy angels. O day of days for the people of God! Then shall the children of the Kingdom shine forth as the noonday sun (Matt. 13:43). The devil subdued and imprisoned, sin eliminated, sorrow past, suffering ended, and tears wiped away! O glorious day! We hail thee from afar! "Even so, come, Lord Jesus" (Rev. 22:20).

15

The Final Judgment

The punishment of impenitent sinners is described in such terrible language that it brings a shudder to every thoughtful soul. That an indescribably horrible doom awaits the sinner who dies without hope in Christ is clearly taught in the Scriptures, and the most graphic descriptions of the torments of the lost are from the lips of the loving Saviour himself. He knew too well to be mistaken. He was too righteous to deceive us. He was too kindhearted to conceal the truth from us and to fail to warn us of the impending doom of the lost.

The whole subject has been beclouded by the failure of the translators of the Authorized Version to distinguish between different Greek words; translating *hades* and *Gehenna* by the word *hell.*

1. THE HEBREW WORD *SHEOL* IS INDISCRIMINATELY TRANSLATED "GRAVE" AND "HELL."

2. THE SEVENTY WHO TRANSLATED THE HEBREW SCRIPTURES INTO GREEK (Septuagint Version—two or three centuries before the coming of Christ), *rendered the Hebrew word Sheol as "hades."* In the Greek New Testament, this word occurs in Matt. 11:23; 16:18; Luke 10:15; 16:23; Acts 2:27,31; Rev. 1:18; 6:8; 20:13, 14. It clearly means "place of departed spirits," both good and bad. It was in two compartments, separated by a great chasm (trans-

lated "gulf" in Luke 16:26). The righteous dead were in paradise, also spoken of as "Abraham's bosom." This designation is from the Talmud. It was adopted by Jesus (Luke 16:22). The reference is to the ancient custom of reclining at feasts, and the place of honor would be next to Abraham, the father of the faithful.

3. PARADISE WAS TRANSFERRED FROM THE UNDERWORLD TO A PLACE NEAR THE THRONE OF GOD.

This change was made at the ascension of our Lord. This seems to agree with Paul's words (Eph. 4:8-10) in which he speaks of the descent of Christ into hades and His ascension, *"carrying captivity captive."* The dead in Christ are absent from the body and present with the Lord (2 Cor. 5:8). Paul was "caught up to the *third heaven . . . into paradise"* (2 Cor. 12:1-4). "Caught up into paradise" shows that paradise had been moved. He desired to depart and be with Christ.

The wicked dead are in *hades,* but not in *hell.* This statement, which is contrary to popular belief, is not made for the purpose of toning down the horrors and sufferings of the impenitent dead, for our Lord describes in the most horrifying words the torments of lost souls in hades. Read again the familiar account in Luke 16:19-31 and the statement that follows (which shows that we are not trying to evade the Bible's teaching concerning future punishment).

4. *GEHENNA* WAS A PLACE IN THE VALLEY OF HINNOM WHERE HUMAN SACRIFICES WERE OFFERED (2 Chron. 33:6; Jer. 7:31). (This Greek word occurs in Matt. 5:22,29,30; 10:28; 18:9; 23:15,33; Mark 9:43,45,47;

Luke 12:5; James 3:6.) In every instance, except the last, the word *Gehenna* falls from the lips of Jesus Christ in the most solemn warning. We identify *Gehenna* and "hell" with the *"lake of fire"* (Rev. 19:20; 20:10, 14, 15). Death and hades are to be cast into the lake of fire. The sufferings of the lost in the lake of fire are described as the second death (Rev. 20:14, 15; 21:8; see also Rev. 20:6). The lake of fire will be the *final prison of the devil,* who will be "cast into the lake of fire and brimstone, where the beast and the false prophet are, and shall be tormented day and night forever and ever" (Rev. 20:10).

5. THE DURATION OF THE PUNISHMENT APPEARS FROM SEVERAL SCRIPTURE PASSAGES TO BE ENDLESS. The words "everlasting fire" (Matt. 25:41), "unquenchable fire" (Matt. 3:12; Luke 3:17), the "fire that never shall be quenched" (Mark 9:43, 45), the "torment" which continues "day and night for ever and ever" (Rev. 20:10), and many other similar expressions force us to hold the view that the punishment of the wicked dead, who share with the devil and his angels in rebellion against God, will likewise share with them in the everlasting fire which was prepared for the devil and his angels (Matt. 25:41).

6. HELL, OR THE LAKE OF FIRE, as intimated in the Scripture verses which we have just quoted, *was not prepared for man,* but for the punishment of the archenemy of God and man, and for the demons which are in league with him. Man goes to hell not by the will of God but against the will of God, who cries out after the sinner, "Turn ye, turn ye . . . for why will ye die?" (Ezek. 33:11).

7. WE CANNOT EXPLAIN, TO THE SATISFACTION OF ALL, THE SEVERITY OF GOD'S ETERNAL JUDGMENT, neither can we fathom His love and mercy to lost sinners who deserve nothing but punishment, and yet through the grace of our Lord Jesus Christ, are exalted to sit with Him in heavenly places (Rom. 11:22; Eph. 2:6). When we see the price paid for our redemption, we know that man's doom without Christ would have been too awful for our feeble words to describe or our imagination to depict. No man is compelled to go to hell, but all are entreated to have mercy on their souls and flee to Christ for refuge. Men do not go to hell because they are sinners, but because they do not want to be saved: "He that believeth on the Son hath everlasting life: and he that believeth not the Son shall not see life; but the *wrath of God abideth on him*" (John 3:36).

"Knowing therefore the *terror* of the Lord, we persuade men" (2 Cor. 5:11). "Now then we are ambassadors for Christ, as though God did beseech you by us: we pray you in Christ's stead, *be ye reconciled to God*" (2 Cor. 5:20).

16

The New Heavens and the New Earth

In a former chapter we dealt with the millennial reign of Christ, but said nothing about the termination of that reign. Paul says that Christ must reign till He has abolished all rule and authority and power and has put all His enemies under His feet. The last enemy to be abolished is death. When this conquest and subjugation of the devil and all his hosts and allies is complete, Christ will then deliver up the Kingdom to God, even the Father (1 Cor. 15:24-28).

As the present age is soon to give way to another age—the Millennium—so the millennial age is to be merged into still another age when God shall be "all in all" (1 Cor. 15:28*)—an age far superior to the Millennium. It is this "age of ages"—or the best and greatest of all the ages— that we are dealing with in this study. Let us try to amplify and clarify this doctrine.

1. AT THE BEGINNING OF THE MILLENNIUM, SATAN IS CAST INTO PRISON AND BOUND FOR A THOUSAND YEARS. At the conclusion of the Millennium, he is "loosed for a little season" and is allowed to deceive the nations and to lead a mighty army

---

*1 Cor. 15:28: "And when all things shall be subdued unto him, then shall the Son also himself be subject unto him that put all things under him, that God may be all in all."

against the saints of God and "the beloved city." Fire is to come down from heaven and destroy this wicked army, and Satan is cast into the lake of fire to be "tormented day and night forever and ever" (Rev. 20:1-10).

2. BEFORE THE MILLENNIUM, ALL OF THE DEAD IN CHRIST ARE RAISED ("the resurrection of life"—John 5:29),[1] living believers are transformed, and both are caught up to meet the Lord in the air (1 Thess. 4:13-17). At the end of the Millennium, the wicked dead will be raised ("the resurrection of damnation"—John 5:29), judged, and cast into the lake of fire to die the second death (Rev. 20:11-15; 21:8).[2] Death and hades will be cast into the same lake of fire (Rev. 20:14). This agrees with Paul's words: "The last enemy that shall be destroyed is death" (1 Cor. 15:26).

---

[1]John 5:29: "And shall come forth; they that have done good, unto the resurrection of life; and they that have done evil, unto the resurrection of damnation."

[2]Rev. 20:11-15; 21:8: "And I saw a great white throne, and him that sat on it, from whose face the earth and the heaven fled away; and there was found no place for them. And I saw the dead, small and great, stand before God; and the books were opened: and another book was opened, which is the book of life: and the dead were judged out of those things which were written in the books, according to their works. And the sea gave up the dead which were in it; and death and hell delivered up the dead which were in them: and they were judged every man according to their works. And death and hell were cast into the lake of fire. This is the second death. And whosoever was not found written in the book of life was cast into the lake of fire.

"But the fearful, and unbelieving, and the abominable, and murderers, and whoremongers, and sorcerers, and idolaters, and all liars, shall have their part in the lake which burneth with fire and brimstone: which is the second death."

118

3. DURING THE MILLENNIUM CHRIST WILL REIGN WITHOUT A RIVAL, while in the age of ages, Christ will deliver up the Kingdom to God the Father, the Supreme Ruler.

4. AS ENOCH, IN THE SEVENTH GENERATION FROM ADAM, LOOKED CLEAR OVER OUR HEADS and saw Jesus coming with His saints to execute judgment (Jude 14, 15), and to usher in the Millennium, so Peter looks clear beyond the Millennium, and sees the destruction of the old order and the appearing of "new heavens and a new earth," characterized by righteousness (2 Peter 3:5-13). John sees the conquest made by the Lord Jesus; His victory over all His foes, including the devil; the resurrection of the wicked dead; and the second-death sentence passed upon them. These things hold his attention until Revelation 21, where he looks past the Millennium and sees the glorious con-summation—the age of ages:

"And I saw a new heaven and a new earth: for the first heaven and the first earth were passed away: and there was no more sea. And I John saw the holy city, new Jerusalem, coming down from God out of heaven, prepared as a bride adorned for her husband. And I heard a great voice out of heaven saying, Behold, the tabernacle of God is with men, and he will dwell with them, and they shall be his people, and God himself shall be with them, and be their God" (Rev. 21:1-3).

5. "HEAVEN AND EARTH SHALL PASS AWAY," said Jesus (Matt. 24:35). Peter says they will "melt with fervent heat" (2 Peter 3:10). This does not mean annihilation; it means the remaking of the material

119

universe, to cleanse it from every stain of sin and to adapt it to new conditions. "Redemption means recovery," said Dr. W. B. Riley, "and that recovery will be complete." Isaiah foresaw this: "Behold, I create new heavens and a new earth" (Isa. 65:17). That the new earth will be superior to the old is certain, for God himself will make it His residence.

6. AS THE STATE OF THE LOST APPEARS TO BE CONTINUALLY WORSE, SO THE STATE OF THE SAVED IS CONTINUALLY BETTER. From a life of sin, sorrow, and defeat, we pass over to a life of peace, joy, and victory. Next we go into a Millennium where golden dreams become real and actual. Then we go with our Lord beyond the Millennium into the new age when God the Father is to be "all in all"—the glorious consummation of the ages, the complete triumph of our God.

7. HUMAN LANGUAGE IS TOO EARTHLY TO DESCRIBE THIS FINAL STATE OF THE BELIEVER. No description of the celestial city could be more gorgeous or resplendent than the word paintings in Revelation 21 and 22. In the letter to the Hebrews, we see that even Abraham, who lived nearly four thousand years ago, by faith looked beyond our time and beyond the Millennium into the age of the ages to an eternal city and kingdom:

"By faith Abraham, when he was called to go out into a place which he should after [afterward] receive for an inheritance, obeyed; and he went out, not knowing whither he went. By faith he sojourned in the land of promise, as in a strange country, dwelling in tabernacles [tents] with Isaac and Jacob, the heirs with him of the same promise: for he looked for a *city which hath foundations, whose builder and maker is God. . . .*

"These all died in faith, not having received the promises, but having *seen them afar off,* and were persuaded of them, and embraced them, and confessed that they were *strangers and pilgrims on the earth.* For they that say such things declare plainly that they seek a country. . . . But now they desire a better country, that is, a heavenly: wherefore, God is not ashamed to be called their God: for *he hath prepared for them a city"* (Heb. 11:8-10,13,14,16).

This is *"the city of the living God, the heavenly Jerusalem,"* "a kingdom which cannot be moved" (Heb. 12:22,28).

8. "EYE HATH NOT SEEN, NOR EAR HEARD, NEITHER HAVE ENTERED INTO THE HEART OF MAN, THE THINGS WHICH GOD HATH PREPARED FOR THEM THAT LOVE HIM. But God hath revealed them unto us by his Spirit" (1 Cor. 2:9,10).

"And I heard a great voice out of heaven saying, Behold, the tabernacle of God is with men, and he will dwell with them, and they shall be his people, and God himself shall be with them, and be their God. And God shall wipe away all tears from their eyes; and there shall be no more death, neither sorrow, nor crying, neither shall there be any more pain: for the former things are passed away.

"And he that sat upon the throne said, Behold, I make all things new. And he said unto me, Write: for these words are true and faithful. And he said unto me, It is done. I am Alpha and Omega, the beginning and the end. I will give unto him that is athirst of the fountain of the water of life freely. He that overcometh shall inherit all things; and I will be his God, and he shall be my son" (Rev. 21:3-7).

Appendix: The Time of the Rapture

1. The snatching of the bride of Christ has come to be known as the Rapture. This word is coming into general use, but is not found in our English Bibles. It comes from the word used in the Latin versions of 1 Thess. 4:17, translating the Greek word meaning to catch or snatch away, and rendered in the Authorized and Revised Standard Versions as "caught up."

2. Until recently, nearly all the Fundamentalists, including the Pentecostals, held that the rapture of the saints is to take place before the Great Tribulation. At a meeting of the General Presbyters of the General Council of the Assemblies of God in 1932, it was reported that in one section of the country certain brethren were teaching that the saints must go through the Tribulation, and with such emphasis, that some assemblies were being disturbed, and some were being divided, and some were withdrawing fellowship from the Council on account of this doctrine. After considerable discussion, the General Presbyters unanimously passed this resolution:

"That we reaffirm our position as being definitely behind the Statement of Fundamental Truths and the declaration therein that we believe in the imminent personal return of our Lord Jesus Christ as the blessed hope of the church, and that we disapprove any of our ministers teaching that the church must go through the tribulation." This was printed and sent to all the Council ministers. At a meeting of the General Presbyters in 1935, the decision of 1932 was reaffirmed.

3. It would take too much space to give an extended argument for the Council's position on this point, but the line of argument is as follows:

a. The word *imminent,* referred to above (used in the Statement of Fundamental Truths—Article 5, Section 13, "The Blessed Hope"), among us has always carried the meaning that the Rapture was near and, so far as we know, may take place at any moment.

Even in the days of Paul, the Church was in an expectant attitude—waiting "for his Son from heaven" (1 Thess. 1:9,10; 1 Cor. 1:7). Paul puts himself in the class with believers who may be on earth at the time of the Rapture: "Then we which are alive and remain . . . " (1 Thess. 4:17). "We shall not all sleep, but we shall all be changed" (1 Cor. 15:51).

The signs of His coming must be fulfilled before Christ's visible appearing, but not necessarily before His secret coming for His saints. And "when these things [the signs of His coming] begin to come to pass, then look up, and lift up your heads; for your redemption draweth nigh" (Luke 21:28). Our redemption is completed at the Rapture; which, as all admit, is still nearer than the revelation or visible coming of Christ.

b. If we put the Tribulation between our time and the Rapture, we cannot look up and lift up our heads or "wait for his Son from heaven"—we will be looking down to see the beginning of the Tribulation. The Tribulation thus may be imminent, but the Rapture is remote—at least, remote enough to follow the Tribulation (which some say is seven years, and some say three and a half). If the Tribulation is not here yet, we cannot now begin "to wait for his Son from heaven," for we know that His coming for His saints is at least three and a half years off, and may be much more. This view cannot be harmonized with the imminency of the Rapture.

c. We do not deny that the saints may go through persecution, for Christ said His followers would be persecuted and that in the world they should have persecution and tribulation (Matt. 10:21-25, 34-36; John 16:33). God's people in several parts of the world are suffering great persecution now. Some are sealing their testimony with their own blood, while others are languishing in dungeons, and still others are wearing their lives away in faraway Siberia. But this is not the Great Tribulation of which our Lord spoke (Matt. 24:21,29).

In Rev. 7:14, the Authorized Version speaks of "great tribulation," but fails to give the full force to the Greek, "the great tribulation" (literally, "the tribulation the great"). This is something more than tribulation such as God's people have had to suffer from the dawn of human history (Heb. 11:33-38). It is from this that the Lord promises to deliver His people: "I also will keep thee from the hour of temptation, which shall come upon all the world, to try them that dwell upon the earth" (Rev. 3:10). "Watch ye therefore, and pray always, that ye may be accounted worthy to escape all these things that shall come to pass, and to stand before the Son of man" (Luke 21:36).

Note: The King James, or Authorized Version, does not capitalize pronouns referring to deity, as is commonly done today. Frequently (though not uniformly) it prints Spirit with a small letter, when the word evidently designates the Holy Spirit. Someone asks how these words read in the Hebrew and the Greek. The Hebrew used all capitals and had no small letters at all. Many of the old Greek manuscripts use uncial or capital letters exclusively, while texts which use both capitals and small letters use capitals very sparingly. Hence, the translators must determine by the meaning of the words and the texts what is proper.

The apparent inconsistency in the use of capitals in this book arises from the fact that different translations are quoted, and the author follows the text quoted—capitalization, punctuation and all—exactly as given, even when his own practice differs from that of the translator or author quoted.